The National Tree-List Layer

USDA FOREST SERVICE

A seamless, spatially explicit tree-list layer for the Continental United States

Stacy A. Drury and Jason M Herynk

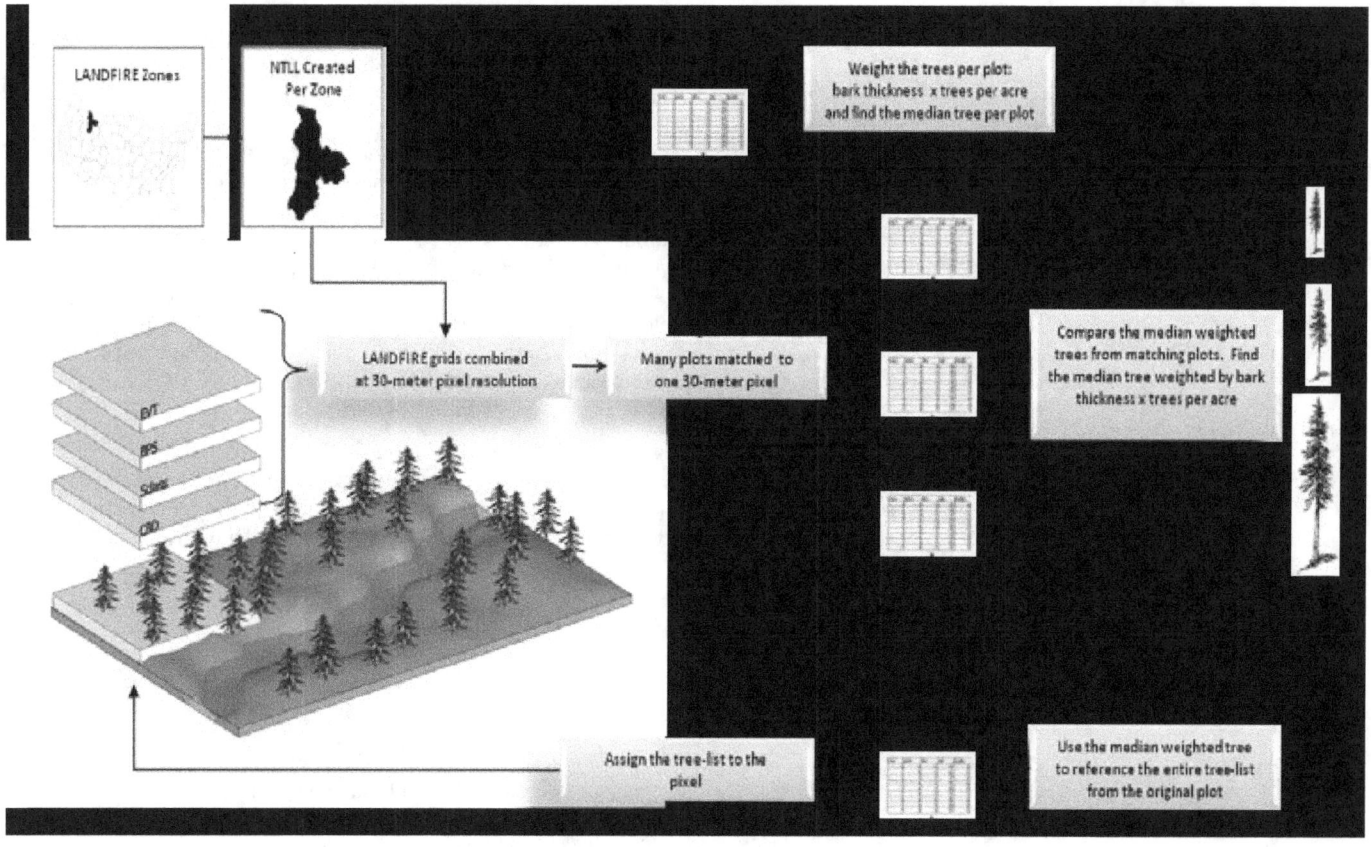

United States Department of Agriculture / Forest Service

Rocky Mountain Research Station
General Technical Report RMRS-GTR-254

February 2011

Drury, Stacy A.; Herynk, Jason M. 2011. **The national tree-list layer.** Gen. Tech. Rep. RMRS-GTR-254. Fort Collins, CO: U.S. Department of Agriculture, Forest Service, Rocky Mountain Research Station. 26 p.

ABSTRACT

The National Tree-List Layer (NTLL) project used LANDFIRE map products to produce the first national tree-list map layer that represents tree populations at stand and regional levels. The NTLL was produced in a short time frame to address the needs of Fire and Aviation Management for a map layer that could be used as input for simulating fire-caused tree mortality across landscapes. Simulated tree mortality estimates using the NTLL as model input provided acceptable results when compared with tree mortality simulations using field-sampled tree attribute data. Our results indicate that fire managers can expect simulated tree-mortalities using the NTLL to predict fire-caused tree mortality as well as field-measured plot data, especially during extreme wildfire events. Decision makers can use tree mortality maps that are produced using the NTLL to develop and support decisions such as where to place fuels treatments or where to most effectively position fire suppression resources.

Keywords: fire hazard, tree-list, LANDFIRE, imputation, nearest-neighbor

AUTHORS

Stacy A. Drury was an Ecologist/GIS Specialist with the Fire, Fuels, and Smoke Program at the USDA Forest Service, Rocky Mountain Research Station's Fire Sciences Laboratory. Currently, he is the Senior Fire Ecologist for Sonoma Technology, Inc. in Petaluma, California. Stacy received his B.S. degree in Terrestrial Ecology from Western Washington University; his M.S. degree in Biological Sciences from Wright State University; and his Ph.D. in Geography from the University of Colorado, Boulder. Stacy has conducted ecology studies in many ecosystems throughout North America. His most current research includes contributing to the Ecosystem Management Decision Support System (EMDS) and the Interagency Fuels Treatment Decision Support System.

Jason M. Herynk is a Programmer Analyst for Systems for Environmental Management. He received his B.S. degree in Geography/Biology from Kansas State University in 2003. He has most recently been involved with the EMDS, Fire Potential Mapping using Fire Program Analysis data, and the LANDFIRE Refresh Project.

You may order additional copies of this publication by sending your mailing information in label form through one of the following media. Please specify the publication title and series number.

Publishing Services

Telephone	(970) 498-1392
FAX	(970) 498-1122
E-mail	rschneider@fs.fed.us
Web site	http://www.fs.fed.us/rm/publications
Mailing address	Publications Distribution
	Rocky Mountain Research Station
	240 West Prospect Road
	Fort Collins, CO 80526

CONTENTS

i   **Research Summary**

1   **Introduction**

4   **Background**

     4   LANDFIRE and the LFRDB

     6   Tree-Lists: Description and Uses

     6   Imputation and Nearest-Neighbor Analysis

7   **Methods**

     7   Overview

     7   LFRDB Vegetation Field Plot Selection

     7   LANDFIRE Map Product Selection

     9   LANDFIRE Map Product Combination

     9   LFRDB Vegetation Plots Assignment to LANDFIRE
              Map Product Combinations

     11   NTLL Evaluation Study Area1

     11   NTLL Map Pixel Assignment Precision

     13   NTLL Comparisons with Independent Vegetation Data

14   **Results**

     14   Vegetation Plot Data Used to Create the NTLL

     15   Nearest-Neighbor Imputation

     15   NTLL Map Pixel Assignment Precision

     15   NTLL Comparisons with Independent Burn Data

20   **Discussion**

     20   Nearest-Neighbor Imputation

     20   Limitations and Known Problems with the NTLL

     21   Management Implications

     23   Future Directions

24   **References**

Research Summary

In 2008, the USDA Forest Service Fire and Aviation Management tasked the Fire Modeling Institute of the Rocky Mountain Research Station to develop a tree population data layer that would be compatible with all other LANDFIRE data layers to simulate tree mortality in fire severity assessments. In this paper, we present the National Tree-List Layer (NTLL) we developed in collaboration with the LANDFIRE project in response to that request. The NTLL is a seamless, spatially explicit geographic information system (GIS) data layer for use as input to calculate fire-caused tree mortality in fire effects simulation models. The NTLL is essentially a digital map that describes tree populations across a landscape. The NTLL describes tree population variability by assigning each pixel within the NTLL a set of field-sampled tree attribute data called a "tree-list." In its most basic form, a tree-list is a list of species, diameters, heights, live crown heights, and densities for every tree on a field-sampled plot. In the NTLL, we further define a tree-list as a geo-referenced table that describes forest structure derived from field-sampled, tree-level plot data that can be quickly accessed by computer programs.

The NTLL was designed to provide fire managers with the inputs needed to compute fire-caused tree mortality using the First Order Fire Effects Model whenever local data for tree populations does not exist within the continental United States. Using a modified version of nearest-neighbor sampling, we imputed geo-referenced vegetation plot data from the LANDFIRE reference database into every pixel of a national-scale digital map to create a spatially explicit, spatially consistent map layer of tree populations. Using LANDFIRE map products, the LANDFIRE reference database, and nearest-neighbor imputation to produce input data for tree mortality modeling proved effective for simulating fire-caused tree mortality during extreme wildfire events. In comparisons with observed wildfire-caused tree mortality, fire-caused tree mortality simulations using the NTLL were within $\pm$ 10 percent of the observed mortality rates when observed crown scorch values were greater than 75 percent. However, tree mortality was consistently over predicted for low intensity wildfires (crown scorch volume <75 percent). Interestingly, simulated tree mortality values using the NTLL were consistent with fire-caused tree simulations using on-site, field-sampled tree attribute data as input data. That is, when input data was provided by the NTLL or derived from field-sample data, fire-caused simulations were in good agreement with wildfire-caused tree mortality ($\pm$ 10 percent) during extreme fire behavior events; however, when fire behavior was low, tree mortality was consistently over predicted. Accuracy for other tree structure attributes such as basal area, density, and crown bulk density (CBD; canopy biomass) was low as percent difference values greater than 100 percent were common. Our results suggest that the NTLL may not be reliable for applications other than fire-caused tree mortality.

Acknowledgments

Funding for this research was provided by the USDA Forest Service, Rocky Mountain Research Station; the Fire Modeling Institute, Missoula Fire Sciences Laboratory; the USDA Forest Service, Fire and Aviation Management Program; Systems for Environmental Management in Missoula, Montana, USA; and Sonoma Technology, Inc. in Petaluma, California, USA. Additional funding was provided by a grant from the Joint Fire Science Program: JFSP-09-1-07-4. We also thank Janet Ohmann, Eric Twombley, James Reardon, and Robert Keane for providing helpful comments on earlier versions.

Sonoma Technology, Inc.

Introduction

The well-documented increase in the number, size, and severity of wildland fires in the western United States over the past decade (Westerling and others 2006) has stimulated government agencies to reduce the intensity and severity of future wildfires in order to protect human life and property (U.S. GAO/RCED 1999; Laverty and Williams 2000; U.S. GAO 2003). Further complicating the issue is the simultaneous increase in the number of humans living near public wildlands throughout the West, thereby creating and expanding a wildland-urban interface (WUI) and increasing the potential for large, severe wildfires to do harm (Radeloff and others 2005; Berry and others 2006; Blanchard and Ryan 2007).

To mitigate the risk and hazard of large, severe wildfires, particularly in the WUI, Federal agencies have advocated fuels reduction treatments (U.S. GAO/RCED 1999; Laverty and Williams 2000; U.S. GAO 2002, 2003, 2005). Although it is debated whether the observed increases in large wildland fire frequency and severity (Westerling and others 2006) are a direct result of decades of fuel accumulation under Federal fire exclusion policies (Brown 1985; Mutch 1994; Ferry and others 1995; Stephens and Ruth 2005) and/or a response to global warming trends that result in longer, drier fire seasons where more fuel is available for burning over longer time periods (Bessie and Johnson 1995; Brown and others 2004; Stephens and Ruth 2005; Running 2006; Westerling and others 2006). It is clear that there are high levels of interconnected wildland fuels that are more frequently exposed to environmental conditions that are conducive to burning; this situation makes fire management difficult. Moreover, of the three main drivers of fire behavior—topography, weather, and fuels—only fuels can be directly managed by fire managers (Rothermel 1972).

To strategically place fuels treatments where they will provide the greatest benefit, fire managers have been charged with developing a detailed methodology for identifying and prioritizing which Federal lands most need fuels reduction treatments (U.S. GAO 2003, 2007; Hessburg and others 2007). An important first step in this prioritization process is to quantify and assess fire hazard, fire risk, and potential fire severity across areas of interest (Hardy 2005).

Comprehensive fire models that quantify fire behavior and effects can be used to provide spatially explicit estimates of fire risk and hazard over a range of spatial and temporal scales (Hessburg and others 2007). However, these risk and hazard assessments must be conducted across large regions with spatial data layers that represent vegetation, fuels, weather, topography, and human settlement (Reynolds and others 2009). While the LANDFIRE project (Rollins and others 2006; Rollins 2009) provides important wall-to-wall fuel maps for fire analyses, one critical layer is missing for calculating comprehensive fire severity assessments—a layer that describes tree population structure that can be used to calculate fire-caused tree mortality (Karau and Keane, in press). In 2008, the USDA Forest Service Fire and Aviation Management (FAM) tasked the Fire Modeling Institute of the Rocky Mountain Research Station to develop a tree population data layer that would be compatible with all other LANDFIRE data layers and that could be used to simulate tree mortality in fire severity assessments.

In this report, we discuss the NTLL we developed in collaboration with the LANDFIRE project. The NTLL is a seamless, spatially explicit GIS data layer for use as input to calculate fire-caused tree mortality in fire effects simulation models. In essence, the NTLL is a digital map that describes tree populations across a landscape (Figure 1). The NTLL describes tree population variability by assigning each pixel within the NTLL a set of field-sampled tree attribute data that is called a "tree-list" (see the example tree-list in Table 1). Tree-lists have been defined either as the tally of individual-tree-level data typically recorded on a forest field plot (species, diameter, height, live crown height, and tree density; Ohmann 2008) or as a list of species and diameters for every tree (Temesgen and others 2003). For our use, a tree-list is a geo-referenced reference table that describes forest structure derived from field-sampled, tree-level plot data (Table 1; Figure 1) that can be quickly accessed by a computer program.

Tree-lists can be used as input to compute tree mortality when local forest structure data are missing or incomplete. This is especially useful when detailed information on potential tree mortality is desired for all lands in an area of interest (Figure 1) but collecting those data is costly and time consuming. The ability to compute potential fire-caused tree mortality is crucial as tree mortality is an important fire effect that is often incorporated into fire hazard and risk analyses. As previously mentioned, land managers and fire simulation modelers often require tree-list data layers to compute fire-caused tree mortality for prioritizing, planning, and implementing many management activities (Jensen and Bourgeron 1993; Haynes and others 2001).

Our objective in creating the NTLL was to produce a seamless tree-list data layer that, when integrated with LANDFIRE map products, could be used to simulate fire-caused tree mortality. We describe how the NTLL was created using a combination of statistical and GIS mapping techniques and a tree-list data set of field-sampled vegetation plots compiled from the LANDFIRE reference database:

- First, we provide background on the LANDFIRE project and the LANDFIRE products that were used to create the NTLL.

- Next, we discuss the statistical and data imputation techniques that were used to assign, or impute, field-sampled vegetation plots to individual pixels within the NTLL.

- Then, we discuss the NTLL validation process.

- Finally, we discuss some possible uses and misuses of the data.

Table 1. Example tree-list data for two vegetation plots from the LFRDB; LANDFIRE Mapping Zone 19.

Vegetation plot identification number	Individual tree identification number	Species	Density (trees/Ha)	Diameter at breast height (cm)	Tree height (meters)	Crown base height (meters)	Canopy class code
19006841	97162	Pinus albicaulis	2.4	16.8	10.1	4.5	codominant
	97175	Pinus albicaulis	2.4	21.6	10.4	4.1	codominant
	97174	Abies lasiocarpa	2.4	12.7	8.2	0.1	intermediate
	97181	Pinus albicaulis	2.4	28.7	10.1	0.5	codominant
	97182	Pinus contorta	2.4	28.4	10.4	4.1	codominant
	97161	Pinus albicaulis	2.4	13.2	9.1	0.9	intermediate
	97173	Pinus albicaulis	2.4	48.8	14.0	1.4	dominate
	97177	Pinus albicaulis	2.4	34.8	9.4	2.2	intermediate
	97176	Pinus albicaulis	2.4	18.5	6.7	0.1	intermediate
	97178	Pinus albicaulis	2.4	21.3	10.1	2.5	intermediate
	97172	Pinus albicaulis	2.4	27.4	11.0	4.4	codominant
	97179	Abies lasiocarpa	30.3	3.0	2.1	0.0	intermediate
	97160	Pinus albicaulis	2.4	23.6	11.0	2.5	codominant
	97169	Pinus albicaulis	30.3	5.3	4.6	2.7	intermediate
	97166	Abies lasiocarpa	30.3	9.7	4.6	0.0	intermediate
	97165	Pinus albicaulis	2.4	29.0	9.1	2.7	codominant
	97167	Pinus albicaulis	2.4	22.9	11.0	4.4	codominant
	97168	Pinus albicaulis	2.4	14.5	5.5	0.0	open grown
	97184	Abies lasiocarpa	2.4	13.5	9.4	2.3	codominant
	97164	Pinus albicaulis	30.3	3.6	2.4	0.0	intermediate
	97163	Pinus albicaulis	2.4	17.0	8.5	2.6	codominant
	97170	Pinus albicaulis	2.4	39.1	11.0	2.7	codominant
	97171	Abies lasiocarpa	2.4	22.4	14.6	3.7	dominate
						0.0	
19004965	86756	Abies lasiocarpa	17.3	7.1	4.3	0.2	codominant
	86759	Pinus albicaulis	0.6	69.1	12.2	1.8	codominant
	86757	Abies lasiocarpa	17.3	10.4	4.9	0.2	codominant
	86755	Abies lasiocarpa	17.3	7.4	4.0	0.2	codominant
	86758	Pinus albicaulis	4.4	24.9	5.2	0.2	codominant
	86750	Pinus albicaulis	0.6	67.8	8.8	0.4	codominant
	86751	Abies lasiocarpa	3.5	27.9	10.7	0.5	codominant

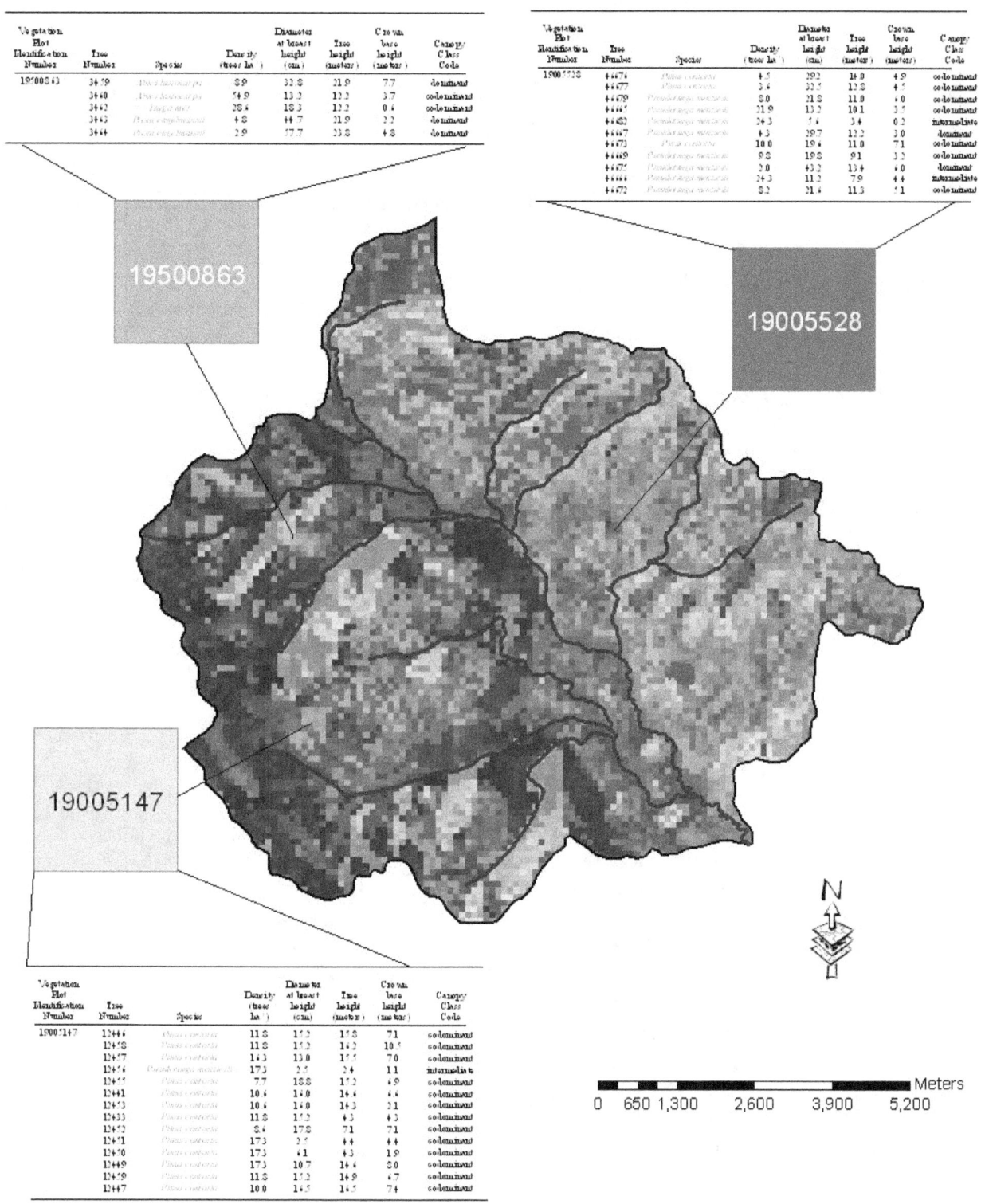

Figure 1. The NTLL coverage for the 8748-ha Placid Creek Watershed, Lolo National Forest, Montana. Each pixel within the NTLL is linked to a set of field-sampled tree attribute data or "tree-list" using a reference number for easy access by computer programs (Table 1). Tree-lists have been defined as the tally of individual-tree-level data typically recorded on a forest field plot (Ohmann 2008). In essence, the NTLL is a spatially consistent compilation of tree population data for an area of interest that serves as input to fire modeling programs.

Background

LANDFIRE and the LFRDB

The NTLL was created using map products from LANDFIRE and the LANDFIRE-Reference Database (LFRDB; Rollins 2009). LANDFIRE was a five-year project to produce spatially consistent, comprehensive digital maps and data products that describe vegetation, wildland fuels, and fire regimes across the United States (Rollins 2009). Chartered in 2004, LANDFIRE was a response to an identified need for comprehensive, geospatial data products to implement Federal wildland fire policy from the local to the national scale (U.S. GAO/RCED 1999; U.S. GAO 2002, 2003, 2005; Rollins 2009). At the heart of the LANDFIRE project is the LFRDB, which is essentially a compilation of all geo-referenced field data available for the continental United States (Rollins 2009) that includes over 800,000 geo-referenced field data plots (Vogelmann and others, in prep). During the creation of the LFRDB, plot data were received from a number of Federal, State, and private sources, including the U.S. Geological Survey Gap Analysis Program, the USDOI National Park Service vegetation monitoring programs, the USDA Forest Service Forest Inventory and Analysis (FIA) program, State national heritage programs, tribal land management agencies, and private institutions (Keane and others 2007; Rollins 2009; www.landfire.gov). Fifty-five percent of the shared field data plots in the LFRDB were contributed by non-Federal organizations (State, tribal, and private institutions), and 45 percent of the contributions came from Federal agencies (www.landfire.gov).

A subset of the vegetation data in the LFRDB is comprised by forest inventory records with detailed measurements of tree attributes such as tree species, diameters, heights (measured or visually estimated), crown ratios, crown position, and tree density (Toney and others 2007; USDA Forest Service 2007). Most of the plot data containing tree-list information were provided by the FIA program, with other contributions from various Federal, State, and private natural resource programs (Table 2). Additional tree and stand attributes needed for fire modeling such as canopy cover, canopy base height, canopy bulk density, and tree height (when not

field measured) were estimated and/or calculated based on field measurements (Monleon and others 2004; Reinhardt and others 2006; Toney and others 2007; Toney and others 2009; Toney and Reeves 2009). All field plots included in the LFRDB were quality controlled by the LANDFIRE team using summary satellite overlays, logic checking, associated metadata, and aerial or ground photos (if available) (Rollins 2009). The LFRDB provided the base from which most LANDFIRE map layers were produced (Rollins 2009).

LANDFIRE map layers were created using a classification and regression tree framework that related the geo-referenced field data in the LFRDB to Landsat imagery and mathematical models (Caratti 2006; Rollins 2009). LANDFIRE map layers used to create the NTLL:

- existing vegetation type (EVT)
- biophysical settings (BpS)
- succession class (SClass)
- crown bulk density (CBD)

The BpS map layer represented the potential dominant vegetation present on the landscape before Euro-American settlement and was based on an approximation of the historical disturbance regime and the current biophysical environment (Rollins 2009). The BpS layer reflected biophysical gradients of site productivity such as present climate, soils, topography, and the competitive potential of native plant species within the context of natural disturbance regimes (Rollins 2009). In the creation of the NTLL, the BpS layer was a simple and effective way to incorporate the complex biotic and abiotic gradients that influenced the presence and absence of vegetation communities. The size, density, and species composition within those communities were criteria in the field plot selection and placement (imputation) process used to map the NTLL (see Methods).

The EVT, the closely related existing vegetation cover (EVC), and the existing vegetation height (EVH) map layers were a set of maps that described existing vegetation composition and structure (Rollins 2009). The EVT described species compositions, the EVC reflected vegetation cover, and the EVH represented vegetation height for a given area

Table 2. Data sources for the LFRDB vegetation plot data used to create the NTLL. Values are number of plots by data source for each regional ecological group. The percent of the total number of plots used to create the NTLL for each regional ecological group is included in parentheses.

Regional ecological groups	LANDFIRE zones	Forest Service[1]	Department of Interior[2]	Other Federal[3]	State[4]	Non-Government organizations[5]	Private[6]	Total number of plots
Pacific Northwest	1, 2, 7, 8, 9	2778 (96.8)	86 (3.0)			5 (0.2)		2869
Pacific Southwest	3, 4, 5, 6	1327 (98.4)					22 (1.6)	1349
Great Basin	12, 13, 16, 17, 18	718 (100.0)						718
Northern Rocky Mountains	10, 19, 20, 21, 22, 29	2523 (97.8)	56 (2.2)					2579
Southwest	14, 15, 23, 24, 25, 27, 28	1313 (100.0)						1313
Texas Southeast	26, 34, 35, 36, 37, 44, 45, 98	985 (100.0)						985
Great Plains	30, 31, 33, 38, 39, 40, 42, 43	318 (100.0)						318
Lake States	41, 49, 50, 51, 52	2314 (100.0)						2314
Appalachia	47, 48, 53, 54, 57, 59	832 (100.0)						832
Southeast	46, 55, 56, 58, 59	1185 (95.0)		8 (0.7)	40 (3.2)	14 (1.1)		1247
Northeast	60, 61, 62, 63, 64, 65, 66	1382 (97.4)	37 (2.6)					1419

[1]"Forest Service" equals data from periodic inventory plots in the USDA Forest Inventory and Analysis Integrated Database, USDA Forest Service Vegetation Surveys, USDA Forest Service plantation inventory plots, published studies conducted by USDA Forest Service Personnel, and FSVeg inventory plot data (www.landfire.gov metadata).

[2]"Department of Interior" data include data from the USDOI Bureau of Land Management Natural Resource Inventories, USDOI Bureau of Indian Affairs Resource Inventories, and the USDOI Geological Survey.

[3]"Other Federal" is data from the Eglin Air Force Base Forest Monitoring program and the National Heritage Programs.

[4]"State" is data from the Florida Division of Forestry's Fire Risk Assessment System.

[5]"Non-Government organization" plot data was provided by The Nature Conservancy.

[6]"Private" data was provided by the Mendocino Redwood Company.

(Rollins 2009; www.landfire.gov). Individual pixels within those vegetation map layers were classified based on the dominant vegetation from the LFRDB field plots using classification and regression tree algorithms that related the field data to Landsat imagery and spatially explicit biophysical gradients (Rollins 2009). In the NTLL creation process, we used the EVT map layers to represent vegetation for a given area, and the EVC and EVH map layers were used by LANDFIRE to create the SClass map layers.

SClass map layers described the successional state of vegetation across the landscape (Rollins 2009). SClass values were mapped by integrating the EVT, EVC, and EVH map layers with the defined vegetation compositions and structural states in the LANDSUM (Keane and others 2006)

vegetation dynamics model (Holsinger and others 2006; Long and others 2006). SClass map layers classified vegetation composition and vertical structure for each of five successional states within LANDSUM (Rollins 2009). In the creation of the NTLL, we used the SClass map layer to further define and integrate species compositions and vertical stand structure into the mapping process.

The CBD map layer in LANDFIRE represented the distribution of canopy biomass across a landscape (Reeves and others 2009; Rollins 2009). To create the CBD layer, crown bulk density values were calculated in FuelCalc (Reinhardt and others 2006) and then mapped using a classification tree approach, Landsat imagery, and the LANDFIRE BpS layer (Keane and others 2006). Within the NTLL mapping process, we used the CBD layer as a criterion for differentiating, selecting, and placing vegetation plots into the map layer based on canopy biomass.

Tree-Lists: Description and Uses

As mentioned earlier, many simulation models require comprehensive, individual- tree-level data in the form of a stand table or tree-list to set the environmental conditions of the area being studied (Eskelson and others 2008). Tree-list data sets have been used as inputs to tree and stand projection models, to update forest inventories, to develop landscape and forest management plans, to assess stand structure at the stand level, and as inputs to wildlife habitat models (Temesgen and others 2003). Several models that are relevant to fire management and that require tree-lists as inputs are the Forest Vegetation Simulator (FVS; Dixon 2002), the Fire and Fuels extension to the FVS (FFE-FVS; Reinhardt and Crookston 2003), FuelCalc (Reinhardt and others 2006), and the First Order Fire Effects Model (FOFEM 5.0; Reinhardt and others 1997).

Imputation and Nearest-Neighbor Analysis

Imputation is a procedure where missing values in a data set are replaced using plausible substitute values (Eskelson and others 2009a, 2009b). Substitute values can be constructed using averaging procedures such as regression models, can be calculated from summary data values, or can be compiled from expert knowledge (Eskelson and others 2009b). However, it is becoming more common to replace missing values in data records or map layers using actual, measured data from the most similar "nearest-neighbor" data record that contains relevant data (Eskelson and others 2009b). Nearest-neighbor imputation has been defined as a set of methodologies where missing or non-sampled measurements for any unit in the population are replaced with measurements from another unit with similar characteristics (Ek and others 1997).

Tree-list data layers are created using nearest-neighbor imputation by comparing reference, or donor, data sets with a target data set or layer. The donor data set is a data source that contains a set of predictor values and a set of response variables (in this case, forest structure attributes) (Ohmann and Gregory 2002; Hudak and others 2008). In the target data layer, only the predictor values are known for each map unit or pixel. Missing information in the target data layer is replaced by matching the predictor values from the reference data set with the predictor values in the target data layer. The response variable information is then inserted, or imputed, into the target data layer. The basic premise underlying nearest-neighbor imputation methods is that data sets with similar predictor values should have similar response values.

Popular nearest-neighbor imputation methods include most similar neighbor (Moeur and Stage 1995), k-nearest-neighbor (Maltamo and Kangas 1998), and gradient nearest-neighbor (Ohmann and Gregory 2002) methods. Each of these imputation techniques uses a set of statistical measures of spectral and environmental characteristics to determine which field-sampled data set is most similar to a target area (pixel) to be mapped (Pierce and others 2009). However, each of these methods differs in how similarities (and differences) between target and reference data sets are assessed, how many neighbors (k) are selected for imputation into a map layer, and how these neighbors are weighted when k>1 (Ohmann 2008).

As noted above, nearest-neighbor imputation methods can use single neighbor plot (k = 1) data to replace missing data values or may use average values for one or more nearest-neighbor plots (k>1) as input data (Eskelson and others 2009a). However, if individual tree-list data such as tree diameters and tree heights are needed as input into tree growth or tree mortality equations, then single plot (k = 1) imputation is required (Eskelson and others 2009b). Moreover, the natural variance in tree populations is lost when tree attributes are averaged across reference plots (Ohmann 2008). In addition, unrealistic forest structures and species assemblages may be produced when reference plot information is aggregated across multiple plots (Moeur and Stage 1995). Single data source (k = 1) nearest-neighbor imputation such as most similar neighbor imputation has advantages over aggregate or averaging techniques (e.g., k-nearest neighbor) in these cases as this technique retains the spatial and attributes variance structures of the data, does not restrict the form or shape of the data distributions, *and* results in data projections that are within the realm of reality for biological systems (Moeur and Stage 1995; Ek and others 1997; Temesgen and others 2003). Increasingly, nearest-neighbor imputation methods are being used to successfully produce comprehensive, spatially consistent tree-list data layers from stand-level field plot data in natural resource management applications (Moeur and Stage 1995; Maltamo and Kangas 1998; Ohmann and Gregory 2002; Temesgen and others 2003; LeMay and Temesgen 2005; Pierce and others 2009).

Overview

To meet our objective of creating a LANDFIRE-compatible, tree-list data layer, we completed the following tasks:

1. Selected geo-referenced forest vegetation plots (tree-lists) from the LFRDB for use as reference data plots in nearest-neighbor imputation.

2. Selected LANDFIRE map products from the LANDFIRE project to represent gradients of ecological processes such as productivity.

3. Combined LANDFIRE map products into a single, searchable combination of the diverse ecological gradients represented by LANDFIRE.

4. Assigned LFRDB vegetation plots (from step 1) to specific LANDFIRE combinations (step 2) to create the nearest-neighbor reference plots (tree-lists) to impute into the NTLL (Figure 2).

5. Located each unique LANDFIRE map product combination (step 3) in the target, NTLL digital map.

6. Imputed the reference plot tree-lists into the NTLL digital map by matching the reference plot map product combination (predictor values) with the LANDFIRE map product combination for each pixel in the NTLL.

7. Selected a single LANDFIRE mapping zone as the NTLL evaluation study area.

8. Evaluated the accuracy and precision of reference plot tree-list placement (step 6) in the completed NTLL within the selected study area.

9. Compared tree mortality predictions with observed fire-caused tree mortality using an independently sampled data set.

LFRDB Vegetation Field Plot Selection

The initial step in creating the NTLL utilized the extensive database of field-sampled, geo-referenced forest vegetation plots from the LFRDB that were organized by LANDFIRE zone. For this study, field plots were selected from the LFRDB by zone if each tree record for a plot had valid values for species, diameter at breast height (DBH), density (individual tree record expanded to represent trees per acre), height, and height to crown base. Throughout this report, we present units in the native units of the data set being described or of the data inputs and outputs for the models being discussed.

LANDFIRE Map Product Selection

In nearest-neighbor imputation, reference plots are inserted into map layers using abiotic and biotic characteristics such as aspect, slope, tree heights, and vegetation composition. Most nearest-neighbor methods use complicated, data-intensive statistical techniques to match the environmental characteristics of reference plots with satellite imagery to fill the target pixels in map layers (Crookston and Finley 2008; Ohmann 2008; Pierce and others 2009). Collecting and processing data needed for these techniques is difficult and time consuming, especially on the national level. We were tasked to produce the NTLL in a short time period; therefore, we turned to the LANDFIRE map products as the only source of environmental data that was readily available, geo-referenced and spatially consistent and that provided coverage for the continental United States.

As previously mentioned, we selected four LANDFIRE map products to represent the complicated environmental gradients that influence the distribution of tree populations across landscapes:

- Species composition. The EVT map layer was selected to represent species composition (see "Background") as the LANDFIRE vegetation layers characterize existing vegetation composition and have been proven useful in various land management applications (www.landfire.gov; Hessberg and others 2007; Keane and others 2010).

- Biophysical environment. The BpS map layer was selected to represent a productivity gradient as the BpS is based on environmental gradients such as climate, soils, and topography (Rollins 2009; see "Background").

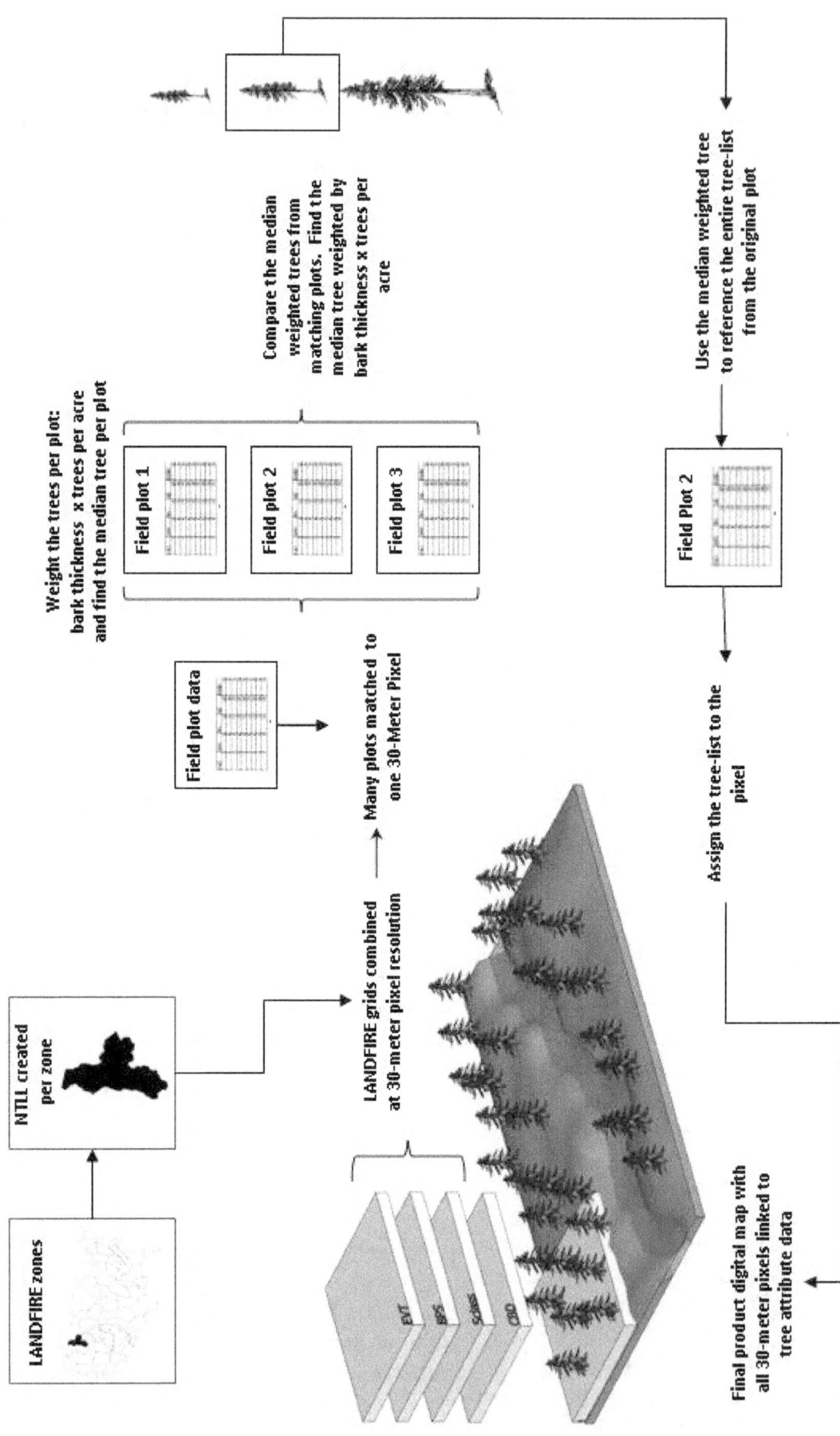

Figure 2. Simplified flow chart of steps used to create the NTLL and the associated look-up table. In this process, LANDFIRE grids (pixels) are combined by EVT/BpS/SClass/CBD code. Next, nearest-neighbor plot data are selected and pooled by grid combination. If more than one nearest-neighbor plot exists for each unique EVT/BpS/SClass/CBD combination, the plot pool is narrowed to a single plot for each grid combination by locating the tree of median bark thickness for each individual plot and then finding the median of all median trees within the grid combination. The plot identity for the median tree is then assigned to that grid combination and to any grid where the grid combination occurs in the mapping zone.

8   USDA Forest Service RMRS-GTR-254. 2011.

- Successional status. The SClass map layer was selected to represent the vegetation successional stage and to directly address stand vertical structure.
- Canopy fuels. The CBD layer was selected to provide information on canopy condition as we felt that the CBD biomass information integrated vegetation health, vegetation composition and structure, and canopy cover into a single metric.

LANDFIRE Map Product Combination

Creating the map product combinations (Figure 2) was the initial step in creating the target map layer that was used during the nearest-neighbor imputation process (described next). First, a target variable map layer was created for each LANDFIRE mapping zone within the continental United States using the Grid to combine functionality in ArcInfo. The EVT, BpS, SClass, and CBD map layers were combined into a single target map layer of predictor values with each pixel containing a single EVT/BpS/SClass/CBD combination (Figure 2). Next, the map product value combinations were exported to a database to facilitate matching the predictor values from the target map layer with the predictor values linked to the LFRDB vegetation plot data.

LFRDB Vegetation Plots Assignment to LANDFIRE Map Product Combinations

In the production of LANDFIRE map layers, each vegetation plot within the LFRDB was associated with a specific pixel or grid value for every LANDFIRE map layer. For example, each vegetation plot had values that were associated with values for EVT, BpS, SClass, and CBD map layers. In our imputation process, we designated the plot values for EVT, BpS, SClass, and CBD as the predictor values for imputation and the tree attribute data for each plot as the response variables (see "Imputation and Nearest-Neighbor Analysis").

Some nearest-neighbor imputation techniques allow for the use of plot data that are averaged over more than one nearest-neighbor plot (k>1; LeMay and Temesgen 2005). However, the NTLL was confined to imputing a single plot (k = 1) into each map pixel because the NTLL was designed to provide input data to simulate tree mortality using the FOFEM 5.0 (Reinhardt 2003), which requires extensive, individual tree data for each plot or stand.

In FOFEM 5.0, the Ryan-Amman algorithm (Ryan and Amman 1994) calculates fire-caused tree mortality probabilities for individual trees over a three-year post-fire interval based on bark thickness and percent crown volume scorched (Hood and others 2007). Inputs for the FOFEM 5.0 application of the Ryan-Amman algorithm include tree DBH (inches), height (ft), live crown ratio, and tree density (trees ha^{-1}; an expansion factor that relates individual trees to number of trees of that size per acre). FOFEM 5.0 calculates the probability that individual trees will be killed by wildfire and also produces outputs for fire-caused tree mortality for an entire stand (total pre-fire number of trees per acre, percent mortality, number of trees per acre killed, average tree diameter of fire-killed trees, and percent mortality for trees greater than 4 inches in diameter (Reinhardt 2003). Since the Ryan-Amman algorithm was developed for use on individual trees, FOFEM 5.0 requires individual-tree-level data that can only be supplied by imputing a single plot for each map pixel.

To ensure that only one vegetation plot was assigned to each map pixel within the NTLL, we first grouped the LFRDB vegetation plots by EVT/BpS/SClass/CBD map product combination (Figures 2 and 3). If more than one vegetation plot was assigned to a map product combination, a single vegetation plot was selected from the plot group for that map product combination using the Statistical Analysis System software (SAS Institute Inc., v. 9.1; Figures 2 and 3) as follows:

- First, bark thickness was calculated for each tree using the algorithms in FOFEM 5.0 (diameter multiplied by a bark thickness coefficient). Trees that did not have a species-specific bark thickness coefficient were assigned an average bark thickness coefficient for the genus. For example, if a *Populus* species coefficient was not found within FOFEM 5.0, an average FOFEM 5.0 code for the *Populus* genus was used to estimate bark thickness.
- Next, the bark thickness coefficient was multiplied by individual tree density values to provide a single metric that could be easily sorted in later processing steps. Bark thickness and tree density were chosen as the selection variables as the tree-lists would be used to simulate tree mortality. Bark thickness is related to the probability of fire-caused tree mortality (Ryan and Reinhardt 1988), and tree density potentially captures the most frequently occurring tree within an area of interest (Figure 3).
- Next, we used the SAS software to identify the median tree per plot using the bark thickness and density metric (Figure 3). We used the median tree per plot to represent each individual plot as we felt that the median would encapsulate the most common, most representative tree

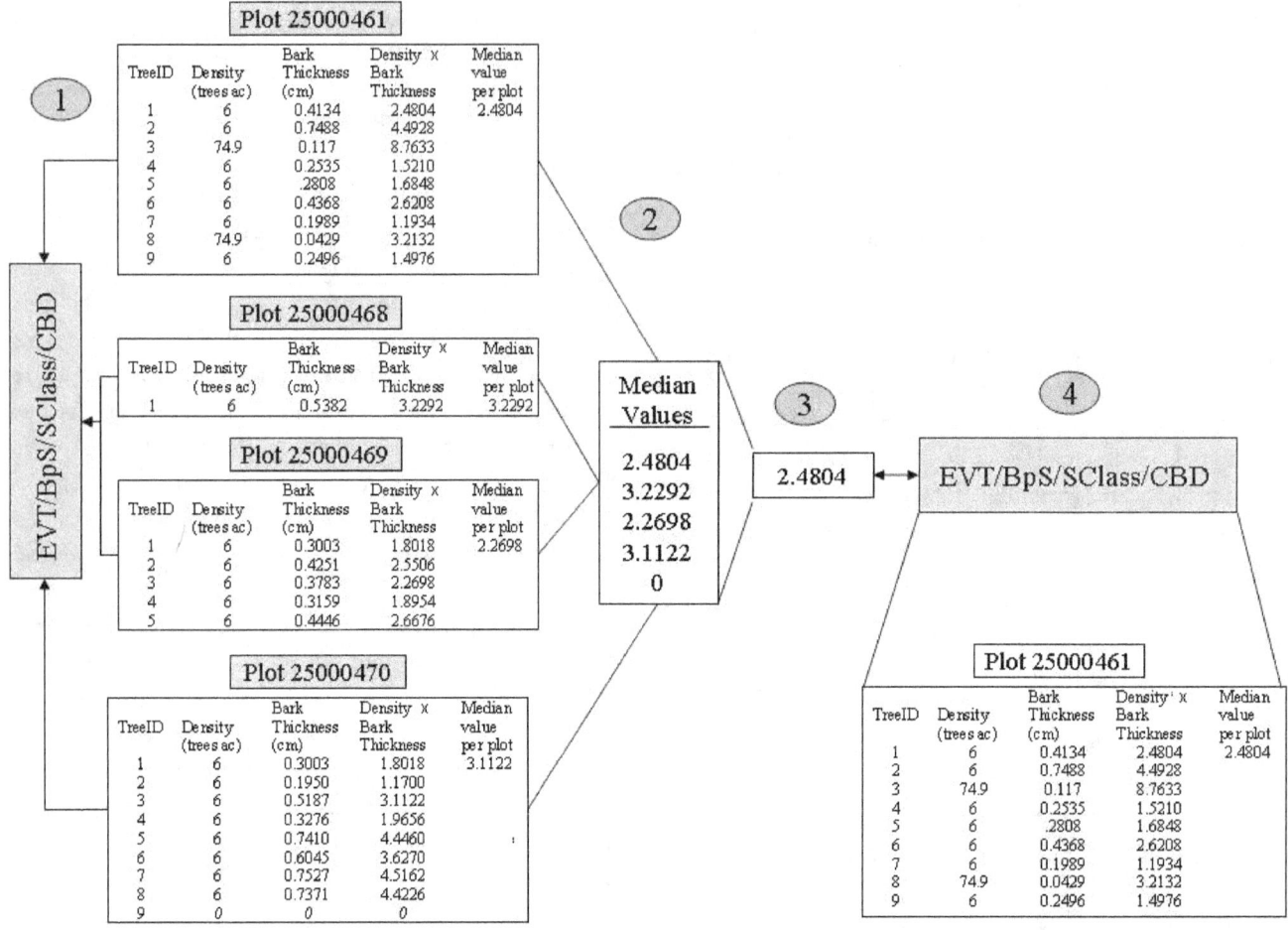

Figure 3. Example flow chart for assigning an LFRDB vegetation plot to a LANDFIRE map product combination. This is a case when four vegetation plots from the LFRDB match a LANDFIRE map product combination. The steps to assign one plot to one LANDFIRE map product combination were:

Step (1): The density and bark thickness coefficient values were multiplied to provide a density-bark thickness metric. MsAccess was used to count the number of tree records on a plot. If there was an even number of records, an extra tree was added with a density and bark thickness of 0 (see tree-list plot 25000470 above) to facilitate determining the median tree record based on the density-bark thickness metric using SAS software—SAS software returns an average for an even number of records (see tree-list plot 25000470). While the mean and average are similar, an average cannot be referenced back to the plot so this approximate median was used. Once median plot values were determined, the median plot values were compared in step (2) to determine the median value of the plot medians (step 3).

Step (2): Median plot values were compared to determine a median value of the plot medians (step 3).

Step (3): The median of the medians value was linked to the original LANDFIRE map product combination.

Step (4): The median value was linked back to the original plot data–in this case, the data for tree-list plot 25000461– and the complete plot data were linked to all pixels in the NTLL target map layer with this LANDFIRE map product combination.

USDA Forest Service RMRS-GTR-254. 2011.

on a plot. Furthermore, the most common tree on a plot based on bark thickness and tree density would best represent the overall tree structure on a plot and the potential magnitude of fire-caused tree mortality within a plot area.

- The plot-level median trees were then grouped by map pixel combination for each unique EVT/BpS/SClass/CBD map pixel combination (Figures 2 and 3).

- The median of the median trees was selected to represent each unique map product combination following the procedure outline above (Figure 3).

- Once a vegetation plot was selected for each EVT/BpS/SClass/CBD map product combination, the complete set of forest structure attributes from the original donor plot was referenced to that map product combination (Figures 2 and 3).

If no vegetation plots within the LFRDB database could be matched to a particular EVT/BpS/SClass/CBD map pixel combination for a particular pixel, a coarser EVT/BpS/SCLASS map pixel combination was used to select a vegetation plot using the median tree selection process previously discussed. If unfilled pixels remained in the targeted map layer, the process was repeated with the EVT/BpS map pixel combination and then again with the EVT map pixel. If a pixel did not contain an EVT code (e.g., not vegetated or not forested) the pixel was coded -9999 to ensure that all pixels in the target map layer were populated. Once all pixels were filled, a forest cover mask from the LANDFIRE project was used to designate forested landscapes as land areas with greater than 10 percent forest cover so that urban or agricultural lands would not be represented as being forested. Then, all lands with less than 10 percent forest cover were designated as non-forest and were not assigned a tree-list.

NTLL Evaluation Study Area

The LANDFIRE Northern Rocky Mountains Mapping Zone 19 (Figure 4; Rollins and Frame 2006) was chosen as the study area to validate the NTLL due to the availability of an independent set of tree attribute data for comparison (Keane and others 2010). The diversity of forest types, the topographical variability within the zone boundaries, and the wide range of elevations covered (760 to 3400 m) by LANDFIRE Mapping Zone 19 (Figure 4) provided a unique opportunity to evaluate the nearest-neighbor strategy used to produce the NTLL. In addition, evaluating the NTLL across forest types provided valuable insights into how effectively the NTLL represented tree structure attributes across the continental United States. For example, within Zone 19, we were able to test the applicability of our tree-list data substitutions in high-elevation alpine communities (~3400 m to timberline); in spruce-fir forests (timberline to 1800 m); and in mid-elevation lodgepole pine, western larch, Douglas-fir, and ponderosa pine forests (Figure 4; Rydberg 1915; Arno 1979).

NTLL Map Pixel Assignment Precision

To evaluate the precision of tree-list map pixel assignment, we compared tree attribute data from the NTLL directly with tree attribute data from the LFRDB at 3042 locations within the study area. This was not an independent test as 758 of the 3042 LFRDB vegetation plots in Zone 19 were used to create the NTLL. However, comparing the tree-list data attributes from the NTLL with the LFRDB plot data provided critical information about the accuracy and precision of plot assignment to individual map pixels using nearest-neighbor imputation and our median tree matching process. Since the nearest-neighbor imputation process used LANDFIRE map product combinations, not latitude and longitude, we felt that it was viable to compare the tree attribute data provided in the NTLL with tree attribute data at the LFRDB plot locations. Moreover, 2284 of the 3042 vegetation plots located within Zone 19 were not used to create the NTLL. Presumably, if the nearest-neighbor imputation process used in this study produced reasonable tree attribute data within the NTLL, then the tree attribute data would be closely matched at each LFRDB plot location by the NTLL.

In this evaluation, we compared how well a specific plot was referenced back to the original plot location in the nearest-neighbor imputation process. To accomplish this task, we needed a single measure that represented each plot and was biologically relevant. The dominant species concept (Cottam and Curtis 1956) was selected for comparison purposes. Species importance values (IV) provide a single metric (percent) based on tree dominance or importance for plot comparisons. Plot importance values are biologically relevant measures that represent tree attribute values similar to the median tree process used in the imputation process as both measures take tree size and tree density into account. Plot importance values for each species (Equation 1) were easy to calculate using the available data.

$$IV = ((species\ relative\ basal\ area + species\ relative\ density) / 2) * 100 \qquad (1)$$

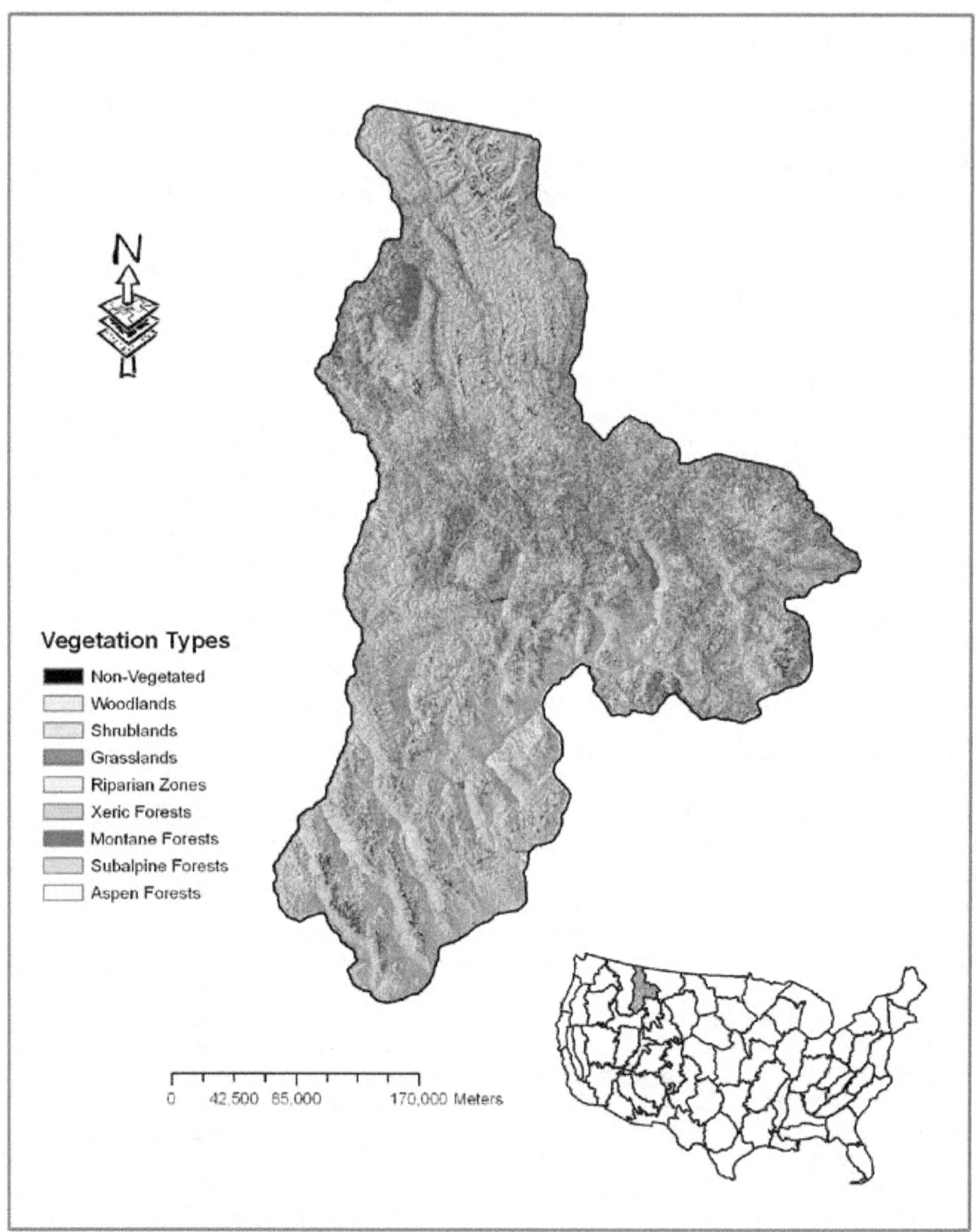

Figure 4. LANDFIRE Map Zone 19; northern Rocky Mountains.

The initial step in this evaluation process was to link tree attribute data from the NTLL to the geo-referenced plot data from the LFRDB. First, we identified the NTLL tree-list plot at each LFRDB plot location. Next, importance values were calculated by species for the LFRDB field-sampled data and the tree attribute data from the corresponding NTLL map pixel. Then, the most important species (based on IV) was selected as the dominant species for each plot.

Percent agreement values were determined by a presence and absence routine where tallies were made of the frequency that the dominant species on the LFRDB vegetation plot matched the dominant species on the NTLL. In addition, frequency tallies were compiled by species each time the NTLL incorrectly represented the dominant species on a field-sampled LFRDB plot.

NTLL Comparisons with Independent Vegetation Data

We also compared the NTLL with a set of independently sampled field plot data. In an earlier model evaluation study, tree structure data was collected on 109, 400-m^2 circular plots within LANDFIRE Map Zone 19 (Keane and others 2010). Forty-nine of the 109 plots were burned during wildfires in 2004 or 2007. This set of geo-referenced field plots was ideal for data comparison with the NTLL as DBH, species, tree height, and fire-caused tree mortality data were collected for each burned and unburned vegetation plot. In addition, this data set was not part of the LFRDB and was not used to create the NTLL.

We tested how well the NTLL served as a data substitute for field-sampled data when predicting tree mortality using FOFEM 5.0. We also tested the efficacy of the NTLL as a data substitute for species dominance, basal area (m^2 ha^{-1}), tree density, and CBD. Determinations of similarity between the independent burn plot data and the NTLL substitute data

were calculated for tree mortality, dominant species presence, basal area, tree density, and CBD using Equation 2. Low percent difference values indicated high percent similarity between the observations and the substitute data within the NTLL. In addition, to identify possible model influences on simulated tree mortality, determinations of similarity were calculated between simulated tree mortality using the NTLL and simulated tree mortality using measured tree attributes as data inputs.

$$((actual-simulated) \, / \, actual) \times 100 \qquad (2)$$

Potential fire-caused tree mortality was simulated using the Ryan-Amman fire-caused tree mortality algorithm (Ryan and Amman 1994), as used in FOFEM 5.0 for all simulations. The Ryan-Amman algorithm calculates tree mortality probabilities for a wide range of species over a three-year post-fire interval based on bark thickness and percentage crown volume scorched (Hood and others 2007). The algorithm predicted that tree mortality would decrease with increasing tree size (increasing bark thickness) and would increase with higher rates of crown scorch (Hood and others 2007). We were able to test the usefulness of the NTLL as a data source for simulating fire-caused tree mortality across a range of fire intensities and burn severities based on the 49 independently sampled vegetation plots that were burned in 2004 or 2007. The variability in burn severities and fire intensities experienced by these plots provided useful information regarding under what conditions simulations of fire-caused tree mortality using the NTLL could be used with confidence.

Additional plot measures of species dominance, basal area (m^2 ha^{-1}), and tree density (trees ha^{-1}) were calculated following standard forest mensuration techniques. CBD values were calculated for all tree-lists using the FuelCalc program (Reinhardt and others 2006).

Results

Vegetation Plot Data Used to Create the NTLL

A total of 15,943 geo-referenced, field-sampled, vegetation plots from the LFRDB were used to create the NTLL (Table 2). A digital map layer with the associated look-up table (NTLL) has been produced for 61 of the 67 LANDFIRE map zones located within the continental United States (Figure 5). The remaining six zones did not contain sufficient tree data to compile tree-lists (Figure 5). Plots were not used across zone boundaries in our imputation process.

Approximately 73 percent of the LFRDB plots included in the NTLL were plots sampled for the USDA Forest Services's FIA program (Reams and others 2005). FIA plot data contributed significantly to every zone mapped during NTLL creation and was the only data source for many mapping zones (Table 2). Other important sources for data garnered from the LFRDB included Forest Service regional forest inventory and monitoring plots, USDOI forest inventory plots, and Florida Department of Forestry Risk Assessment plots (Table 2).

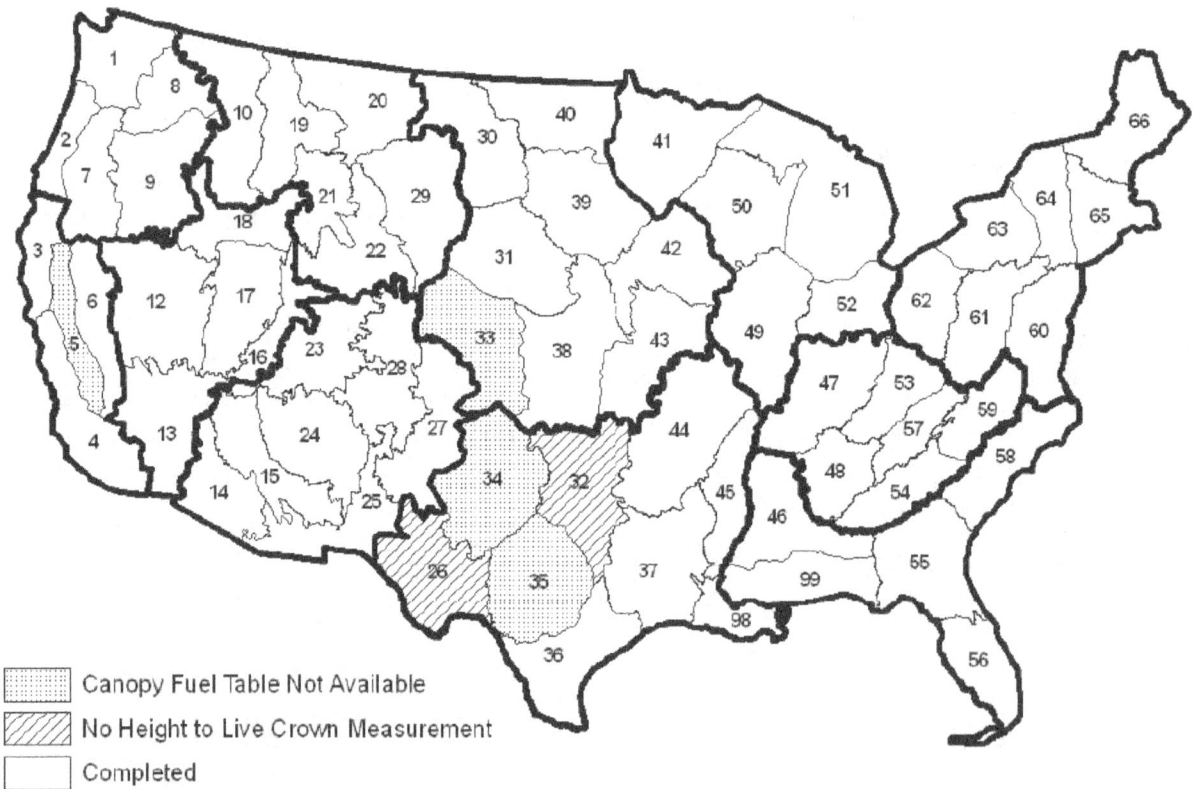

Figure 5. LANDFIRE mapping zone locations. The NTLL provides tree population information (tree-lists) for 61 of the 67 LANDFIRE mapping zones within the continental United States. The NTLL data layer was not completed for the six remaining zones due to inadequate data sources, that is, there was no canopy fuel information or height to live crown measurements did not exist.

Nearest-Neighbor Imputation

In the nearest-neighbor imputation process, field-sampled plot data were successfully matched and imputed to target pixels in the NTLL using the most stringent EVT/BpS/SClass/ CBD predictor variables on 73 percent of the target map pixels (Table 3). An additional 2 percent of the 30-m target pixels were assigned tree-list plots using the less stringent EVT/BpS/ SClass predictor variables (Table 3). Of the remaining map pixels, 7 percent were assigned tree-list plots based on the EVT/SCLASS combination, and 18 percent were filled based solely on the EVT (Table 3).

There is likely an east-west difference in imputation accuracy for the NTLL as the quality of the imputed map layer is likely dependent on the number of LFRDB plots within a LANDFIRE mapping zone, and there were far more LFRDB vegetation plots available in the western LANDFIRE map zones than in the eastern LANDFIRE map zones (Table 3). This geographical bias in the NTLL is shown by the frequency of map pixel imputation using the most rigorous, and presumably most accurate, nearest-neighbor imputation strategy where the complete EVT/BpS/SClass map product combination is used to assign LFRDB plots to individual map pixels (Table 3). For example, Zone 1 (Northern Cascades) is 70 percent forested, 1008 LFRDB field plots were used in the NTLL, and 84 percent of the target map pixels were filled using the EVT/BpS/SClass/CBD combination to link the reference data to the target pixels (Table 3). In contrast, Zone 36 (the Western Gulf Plains) is an example of where the NTLL is presumably less accurate as only seven vegetation plots where available to create the tree-list map layer (Table 3). With few vegetation plots available, 53 percent of the forested pixels within Zone 36 were assigned to NTLL map pixels based solely on the EVT data layer (Table 3).

NTLL Map Pixel Assignment Precision

Dominant species presence based on species IV was accurately matched in the NTLL at 61.7 percent of LFRDB plot locations within the Zone 19 study area (Table 4). The NTLL best served as a data substitute for field-sampled data at LFRDB plot locations where *Pseudotsuga menziesii*, *Pinus contorta*, and *Abies lasiocarpa* were identified as dominant species based on high species IV (Table 4). These three forest types were well represented within the LFRDB (77.6 percent of the 3042 LFRDB vegetation plots) and were accurately matched based on dominant tree species presence by the NTLL at 71.8 percent of the *Pseudotsuga menziesii* plot locations, 62.2 percent of the *Pinus contorta*

plot locations, and 70.1 percent of the *Abies lasiocarpa* plot locations (Table 4).

However, the NTLL did a less favorable job of simulating dominant species presence for forest vegetation types that were represented less frequently within the LFRDB and presumably occurred less frequently within the Zone 19 study area (Table 4). For example, when *Pinus ponderosa* or *Picea engelmannii* were the dominant species in the LFRDB plots, the percent agreement values fell to 35.8 and 24.0 percent. Moreover, *Pseudotsuga menziesii* plot data were often assigned to map pixels where the field data indicated that *Pinus ponderosa* or *Picea engelmannii* were dominant species (Table 4).

NTLL Comparisons with Independent Burn Data

Tree-List Map Pixel Assignment. Similarity in dominant species composition was considerably lower between the independently sampled vegetation plots and the NTLL (Table 5). For example, the dominant species was matched by the tree-list plots on only 27.5 percent of the 109 independently sampled plots (Table 5). Moreover, 24 of the 109 independently sampled plot locations were falsely designated as non-forested (forest cover equals less than 10 percent). The only locations with moderate agreement between the paired plots (51 percent dominant species match; Table 5) were the *Pseudotsuga menziesii*-dominated independent plots. Moreover, there was a tendency to favor assigning *Pseudotsuga menziesii*-dominated tree-list plots to most forested map pixels during the imputation process as 48 percent of the 85 plot locations that were assigned tree-list plot data in the NTLL were assigned to *Pseudotsuga menziesii* (Table 5).

Tree Mortality. Wildfire-caused tree mortality was observed on 49 of the independently sampled plots across a range of fire intensities and fire severities. In comparisons between the observed wildfire-caused tree mortalities and our predicted tree mortality rates using the NTLL as model input (Table 6), we inferred that tree mortality was predicted well (>20 percent agreement) under conditions where high tree mortality rates were observed (crown scorch volumes>75 percent), and it was poorly predicted when observed mortality rates were low or moderate (Figure 6a). At low crown scorch volumes (<10 percent), the errors in tree mortality predictions were potentially large, but no systematic tendencies to over or under predict tree mortality were observed (Figure 6a). However, in the mid-ranges for crown volume scorched (10 to 75 percent crown volume scorched), tree mortality tended to be over predicted using the NTLL for model inputs (Figure 6a).

Table 3. Summary statistics for the LFRDB and tree-list imputation into the NTLL.

				Percent of grids			
Zone number	Land area (km²)	Percent forested	Number of tree-list plots[1]	imputed using the EVT/BpS/ SClass/ CBD code	imputed using the EVT/BpS/ SClass code	imputed using the EVT/BpS code	imputed using the EVT code
1	10,458,606	70	1008	84	3	11	3
2	5,324,294	70	419	71	6	11	12
3	6,222,699	54	417	81	5	10	4
4	12,913,188	14	204	45	1	10	44
6	8,785,268	65	728	83	4	9	4
7	9,889,513	69	1106	74	4	11	11
8	8,208,849	4	37	9	2	12	78
9	15,406,458	27	299	57	15	16	13
10	15,192,580	68	927	88	3	6	4
12	19,669,971	16	105	75	0	15	10
13	14,946,699	2	22	61	0	32	7
14	9,976,483	1	6	75	0	22	3
15	11,669,907	47	360	79	2	12	7
16	6,994,990	58	410	76	2	6	15
17	12,844,075	19	107	64	0	24	11
18	10,143,353	10	74	61	4	14	21
19	11,485,702	46	758	67	2	18	13
20	14,101,521	8	83	89	1	8	2
21	8,171,429	49	529	78	4	6	11
22	13,300,507	7	71	70	1	10	18
23	13,425,426	30	173	78	1	12	9
24	14,123,473	25	163	78	4	12	6
25	12,167,867	16	110	55	2	6	37
27	14,543,646	10	131	77	1	5	17
28	14,974,632	63	370	80	2	8	11
29	17,160,718	16	211	90	0	5	5
30	14,828,554	5	18	90	0	1	9
31	15,892,482	3	63	69	0	0	30
36	14,977,186	17	7	32	0	15	53
37	18,047,902	67	474	84	4	3	9
38	19,896,141	62	50	48	0	1	51
39	16,475,652	1	11	29	0	0	70
40	13,497,207	4	52	85	0	1	13
41	18,082,256	53	746	87	2	5	7
42	13,795,547	9	46	47	0	1	51
43	14,939,061	15	78	21	0	0	8
44	21,270,482	59	361	78	2	5	16
45	8,882,174	24	82	85	3	2	10
46	13,546,360	64	154	73	2	4	20
47	15,374,463	45	132	69	0	3	27
48	8,435,206	59	210	74	1	5	19
49	17,160,362	16	193	46	0	2	52
50	14,757,433	40	529	82	2	3	13
51	25,276,664	32	792	90	1	1	8
52	9,180,766	9	54	16	0	1	83
53	8,426,198	74	19	87	2	5	7
54	8,749,780	71	138	92	2	1	5
55	15,616,751	66	461	65	24	6	5
56	9,951,061	26	134	47	12	24	17
57	6,258,763	75	185	84	1	4	11
58	12,134,657	55	314	91	1	4	4
59	8,304,874	61	148	92	1	2	5
60	11,670,646	41	238	73	1	4	22
61	11,767,503	68	251	87	1	3	9
62	9,747,225	53	131	71	1	4	25
63	9,366,589	52	163	81	2	4	12
64	8,527,765	69	195	72	2	9	17
65	8,773,276	54	155	74	4	6	17
66	12,704,376	76	286	86	2	6	7
98	5,872,113	23	61	80	4	6	10
99	11,127,584	63	184	82	2	5	11
All zones	8,504,632,386	37	15943	73	2	7	18

[1]Selected from the LFRDB.

Table 4. Comparisons of dominant species presence at 3042 LFRDB plot locations within LANDFIRE Zone 19 and dominant species presence at the same locations in the NTLL. Dominant species per plot was determined using importance values (Cottom and Curtis 1956). Table should be read similar to mileage charts in road maps. For example, *Pseudotsuga menziesii*-dominated plots in the LFRDB are commonly represented by *Pseudotsuga menziesii*-dominated plots in the NTLL (71.8% agreement). However *Pseudotsuga menziesii*-dominated plots are rarely misrepresented by *Pinus ponderosa*-dominated plots (1.5% occurrence). Yet *Pinus ponderosa*-dominated plot locations from the LFDRB are misrepresented by *Pseudotsuga menziesii*-dominated plots in the NTLL at 42.3% of the plot locations.

Dominant species recorded plot within the LFRDB	Number of LFRDB plots	Percent of total number of LFRDB plots	Percent agreement between tree-list and FIA plots with the following dominant species designations:							
			Pseudotsuga menziesii	*Pinus contorta*	*Abies lasiocarpa*	*Picea engelmanni*	*Pinus ponderosa*	*Pinus albicaulis*	*Larix occidentalis*	*Others*
Pseudotsuga menziesii	1119	36.8	**71.8**	7.1	5.2	3.5	1.5	0.9	0.5	9.5
Pinus contorta	680	22.4	16.0	**62.2**	8.8	3.2	0.6	1.0	0.4	7.8
Abies lasiocarpa	561	8.4	8.7	11.1	**70.1**	3.7	0	3.0	0	3.4
Picea engelmannii	167	5.5	18.0	13.8	31.1	**24.0**	1.2	3.6	0	8.3
Pinus ponderosa	137	4.5	42.3	4.4	2.2	0.7	**35.8**	0	0.7	13.9
Pinus albicaulis	105	3.5	0	14.3	41.0	1.0	0	**34.3**	0	9.4
Larix occidentalis	95	3.1	21.1	17.9	14.7	5.3	3.2	0	**26.3**	11.5
Others	153	5.0	12.4	11.1	9.8	2.0	0.7	1.3	2.0	**56.9**
Totals	3042	100	**Total percent matched correctly = 61.7%**							

Table 5. Comparisons of dominant species presence at 109 field-sampled plot locations within LANDFIRE Zone 19 and dominant species presence at the same locations in the NTLL. Dominant species per plot was determined using importance values (Cottom and Curtis 1956). Table should be read similar to a mileage chart in a road map (see example in Table 4).

Dominant species on plot	Number of plots	Percent of total number of plots	Percent of independent field plots assigned tree-lists with the following dominant species:							
			Pseudotsuga menziesii	*Pinus contorta*	*Pinus ponderosa*	*Larix occidentalis*	*Abies lasiocarpa*	*Picea engelmanni*	*Others*	*>10% forest*
Pseudotsuga menziesii	41	37.6	**51**	10	5	2	7	2	7	15
Pinus contorta	30	27.5	23	**17**	7	3	10	10	3	27
Pinus ponderosa	12	11.0	58	8	**8**	0	0	0	0	25
Larix occidentalis	10	9.1	30	10	10	**0**	0	0	0	50
Abies lasiocarpa	9	8.3	22	11	11	0	**22**	0	11	22
Picea engelmannii	7	6.4	43	0	0	0	14	**29**	14	0
Totals	109		100 **Total percent matched correctly = 27.5%**							

Table 6. Evaluation of fire-caused tree mortality (%) comparing simulated fire-caused tree mortality with observed tree mortalities (%) on 49 plots burned by wildfires in 2003 and 2007.

No difference[1]	Difference ≤10%	Difference ≤25%	Mean absolute error[2]	Mean square error (rmse)
NTLL simulated tree mortality compared with observed tree mortality				
n = 10 (20)	n = 27 (55)	n = 29 (59)	23 (6, 0, 25, -18.5)	1105 (33)
Simulated tree mortality using field-sampled tree attribute data compared with observed tree mortality				
n = 11 (22)	n = 20 (41)	n = 29 (59)	25 (20, 0, 26, -22.6)	1249 (35)
Simulated tree mortality using field-sampled tree attribute data compared with simulated tree mortality using the NTLL				
n = 27 (55)	n = 30 (61)	n = 36 (73)	15 (0, 0, 22, 4.1)	702 (26)

[1] Percent of total number of plots in parentheses.
[2] Units are percentage points. Mean absolute error is simply the mean of the absolute value of the errors. Median, mode, standard deviation, and a bias measure are in parentheses. Bias is evaluated by taking the mean of the errors without transformation.

Similar trends were noted when the observed wildfire-caused tree mortalities were compared with simulated tree mortalities using the on-site, field-sampled tree attribute data as inputs into the tree mortality model (Table 6; Figure 6b). Tree mortality was predicted well when crown volume scorch was more than 75 percent, and it was consistently under predicted when crown scorch volume was less than 75 percent (Figure 6b).

When we compared the tree mortality simulations using the field-sampled data and the NTLL directly (Table 6), there was no difference among the 22 of the 24 simulations that were conducted under high fire severity conditions (>75 percent crown scorch volume; Figure 6c). However, in low and moderate severity conditions (<75 percent crown volume scorched), there was little agreement between the simulated tree mortalities using the NTLL and the field-sampled data sets for model input as the percent difference values ranged from 0 to $\pm$ 80 percent (Figure 6c).

Basal Area, Tree Density, and CBD. Basal area, tree density, and CBD on the independently sampled plots were poorly mapped by the NTLL. Percent difference was greater than 50 percent for the basal area comparisons on 62 percent of the 77 field plots available for testing, and difference exceeded 100 percent on 21 percent of the plots. In addition, the results of a Freese chi-square accuracy test also suggested that large potential errors exist when using the NTLL to represent basal area as the test was not significant ($\alpha = 0.05$) until an error of 36 m^2 ha^{-1} was accepted—a basal area value higher than the measured basal area on 65 of the 77 field-sampled plots.

The NTLL also poorly represented tree density as the percent differences in density were greater than 50 percent on 59 of the 77 independently sampled plot locations. In addition, the mean absolute error was high for tree density (MAE = 989 trees ha^{-1}) and the Freese statistic was not significant ($\alpha = 0.05$) until we accepted an error of 2800 trees ha^{-1}—an error value that exceeded the measured tree densities on all 77 field plots. Finally, CBD was poorly predicted as less than 36 percent of the independently sampled plots were represented adequately (<25 percent difference) by the NTLL.

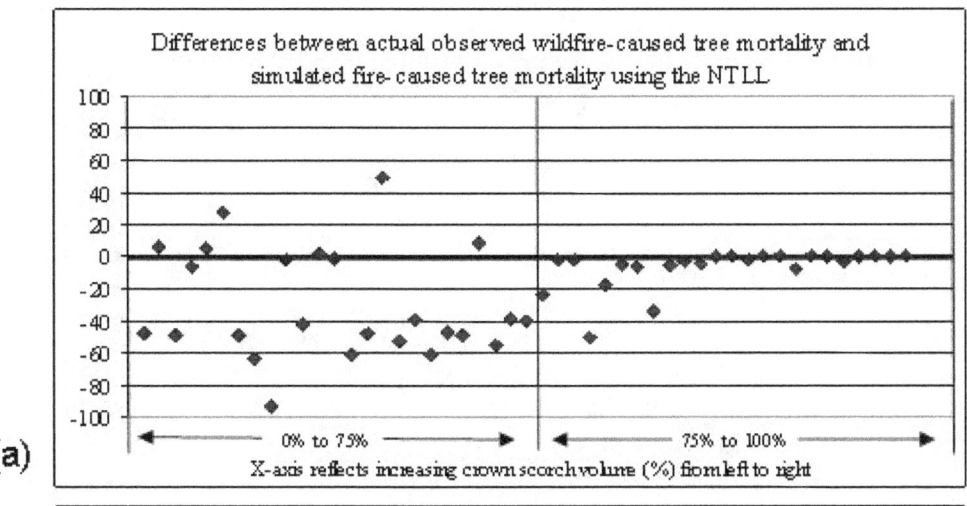

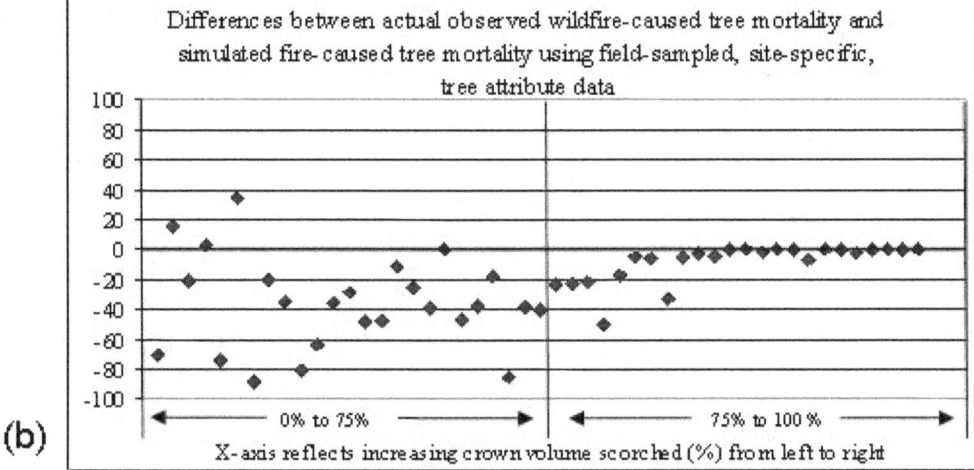

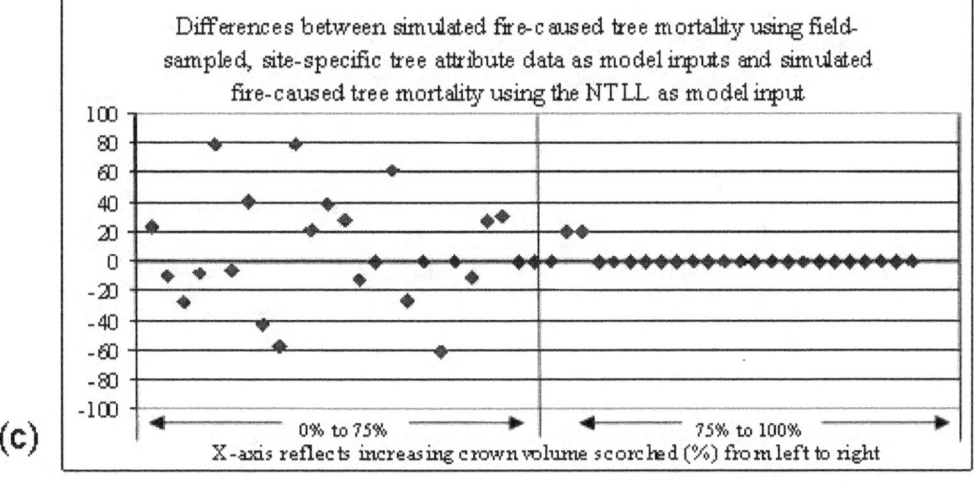

Figure 6. Comparisons among observed wildfire-caused tree mortalities and Ryan-Amman model results using the NTLL and field-sampled, site-specific tree attribute data as model inputs. Model input variables were bark thickness and observed crown volume scorched (percent). (A) illustrates the differences between actual, observed wildfire-caused tree mortality and simulated fire-caused tree mortality using the NTLL as Ryan-Amman model input. (B) shows the differences between actual wildfire-caused tree mortality and simulated mortality using field-sampled tree attribute data from each of the burned vegetation plots as model input. (C) summarizes the observed differences between model simulations using the NTLL as model input and using the field-sampled tree attribute data as model input.

Discussion

The NTLL is a good first approximation of a national-scale, spatially explicit, spatially consistent set of substitute tree attribute data that could be used to simulate fire-caused tree mortality. While improvement is needed, the reasonable agreement between the observed fire-caused tree mortalities and the simulated fire-caused tree mortalities indicates that fire managers and modelers can expect simulated tree mortalities using the NTLL to perform as well as field-measured plot data in predicting fire-caused tree mortality, especially during extreme wildfire events (Figure 6).

Nearest-Neighbor Imputation

The relatively good fit between the NTLL data layer at the LFRDB plot locations in Zone 19 indicates that our nearest-neighbor imputation process assigned biologically relevant reference data to the appropriate locations in the map layer. This test may be viewed as more of a test of nearest-neighbor imputation precision than a test of imputation accuracy. That is, 758 of the 3042 LFRDB plots available for Zone 19 were used to create the NTLL; so for those 758 locations, we were testing how well the plots were reassigned to their true field locations. However, this test also provided some insight into how accurately the NTLL represented actual vegetation compositions across the landscape as more than two-thirds of the LFRDB vegetation plots available in Zone 19 (2284 of 3042) were not used to create the NTLL. Moreover, we did not know the locations of the LFRDB plots, so latitude and longitude values were not used to assign vegetation plots in the NTLL. All vegetation plots were assigned to map pixels using the LANDFIRE map products to represent environmental gradients in nearest-neighbor imputation. So if any of the 758 vegetation plots were assigned to their initial landscape positions in the NTLL, this was done entirely by using LANDFIRE map production layers to predict where to place the plots in the map layer. This indicates that the LANDFIRE map products can be used effectively as the predictor values needed to assign reference plots to similar areas in target areas.

Limitations and Known Problems with the NTLL

The poor representation of basal area, tree density, and CBD using the NTLL is a concern. Although the NTLL was not built specifically to serve as a map layer that represents basal area, tree density, or CBD, we hoped for better agreement than was observed. As we discussed previously, NTLL accuracy may improve as LANDFIRE is improved, or alternative queries using other LANDFIRE map products may result in a more accurate NTLL. The power of our technique that uses the LFRDB and LANDFIRE map products is that additional tree-lists can be compiled and evaluated to address specific needs with relatively little time and effort. A goal of future NTLL development may be to investigate how to improve the tree population data contained in the NTLL to the point where the NTLL has universal applications. That is, to produce a national tree-list map layer that is universally useful for a wide range of applications such as tree growth and yield models, succession models, and wildlife habitat in addition to fire-caused tree mortality modeling.

An additional problem we found when comparing the NTLL with the independently sampled plots was that some areas where we knew that trees were present were labeled as non-forested and were not assigned a tree-list. However, this mapping error may be a result of the forest mask used, in which only forested cover types that had greater than 10 percent cover were assigned a tree-list—this could be fixed by using a different mask or assigning a lower percent cover value to the forest mask.

Another concern is that we do not present any map validation results outside of Zone 19. The short time frame imposed on this project by FAM and the limited resources we had to complete the work precluded a detailed map validation effort for the entire NTLL coverage area. Moreover, other studies have documented low accuracies (<50 percent) for LANDFIRE map layers (Holsinger and others 2006; Rollins and others 2006; Keane and others 2010), and we felt that the accuracy of the NTLL would be entirely dependent on the LANDFIRE map products. Moreover, we did not have easy access to other independently sampled, geo-referenced data sets outside of Zone 19. Since we used LFRDB vegetation plot data to create the NTLL, we felt that a true validation of the NTLL required independently sampled plot data for comparison purposes. We suggest that a map validation of the entire NTLL coverage area would probably reflect the accuracies we computed for Zone 19.

A final critique is that our nearest-neighbor assignment technique using the median tree to assign LFRDB vegetation plots to combinations of LANDFIRE map products may reduce the variability present in the NTLL. Pierce and others (2009) discuss how the choice of methods for plot selection and weighting influences local, plot-level prediction accuracy and regional representations of tree populations. Our exclusive use of median conditions to choose vegetation plots in the nearest-neighbor plot selection process may mean that we improve local accuracy, which we assessed in this report, at the expense of adequately representing regional tree populations. This was not an issue in our production of the NTLL as we were interested in improving the effectiveness of the NTLL at the local stand level. However, more work needs to be done to investigate how to minimize these tradeoffs between local and regional scale accuracy so that future tree-list map layers emphasize which type of accuracy—local or regional—is more important based on the projected uses of the map product.

Management Implications

In the context of increasingly longer, more severe fire seasons (Westerling and others 2006), fire managers need decision support tools that help identify where the greatest risk of adverse fire effects exist across landscapes. Managers are particularly concerned about fire-caused tree mortality. The NTLL is a potentially useful decision support tool that provides reasonable simulations of regional, fire-caused tree mortality, especially under extreme conditions. However, our results indicated that fire-caused mortality simulations under less extreme burning conditions should be viewed with caution as the Ryan-Amman algorithm overestimated tree mortality using field-sampled tree attribute data and the NTLL when fire behavior potentials were low.

Another concern of a national tree population layer such as the NTLL is whether the tool is useful at the local scale (Pierce and others 2009). Our results indicated that the NTLL provided acceptable results at the local scale. When used in combination with other LANDFIRE products and local knowledge, the NTLL provided useful information regarding fire-caused tree mortality for local management decisions. The

simulated fire-caused tree mortality values we calculated were compatible with the tree mortality simulations calculated using field-sampled plot data for individual stands. Nevertheless, it is likely that local data will provide more accurate results as the NTLL has the potential to misrepresent tree attribute data at a single point. Land managers and fire modelers should use local, field-measured stand data when available.

We do not recommend using this version of the NTLL for planning purposes that require accurate representations of stand basal area or density as the NTLL was developed specifically as an input for the Ryan-Amman tree mortality algorithm. Rather, tree-lists that provide more accurate representations of the variables of interest should be constructed once specific needs are identified. A strength of our process is that new tree-list map layers that seek to represent specific forest structure attributes can be created under short time frames by modifying the search and imputation process to address specific needs.

The most obvious use of the NTLL is for long-term strategic planning to mitigate possible adverse fire effects such as unwanted tree mortality. In Figure 7, we show how fire-caused simulation results can be used by decision makers who are tasked with locating fuels treatments and or the strategic placement of fire suppression resources. Figure 7 summarizes the results of tree mortality simulations, potential for crown fire simulations, and potential fuel consumption using the FIREHARM fire modeling platform (Keane and others 2010). Although the simulations presented here were conducted to assess fire hazard and fire risk in the Lower Placid Creek watershed in western Montana, this modeling approach can be applied to any size landscape of interest. The premise shown is that, using these tools, a fire manager can develop a long-term plan for assessing where to station fire suppression resources or to locate fuels treatments in order to lower the likelihood of undesirable fire effects such as high tree mortality. For example, along the western ridge of the Lower Placid Creek watershed, the potential for crown fire is high (>75 percent) throughout the 120-day fire season (June through September; Figure 7a; Keane and others 2010). Coupled with the average fuel consumption potentials shown (Figure 7b), it is clear that tree mortality would likely be high (as indicated in the simulations; Figure 7c). If a fire management goal was to contain potential crown fires within the Lower Placid Creek watershed or to lower the possibility of excessive tree mortality within the watershed, fire managers would logically locate fuels treatments in the western third of Lower Placid Creek and/or place fire suppression resources in favorable positions to minimize the potential of fire escaping the watershed from the west.

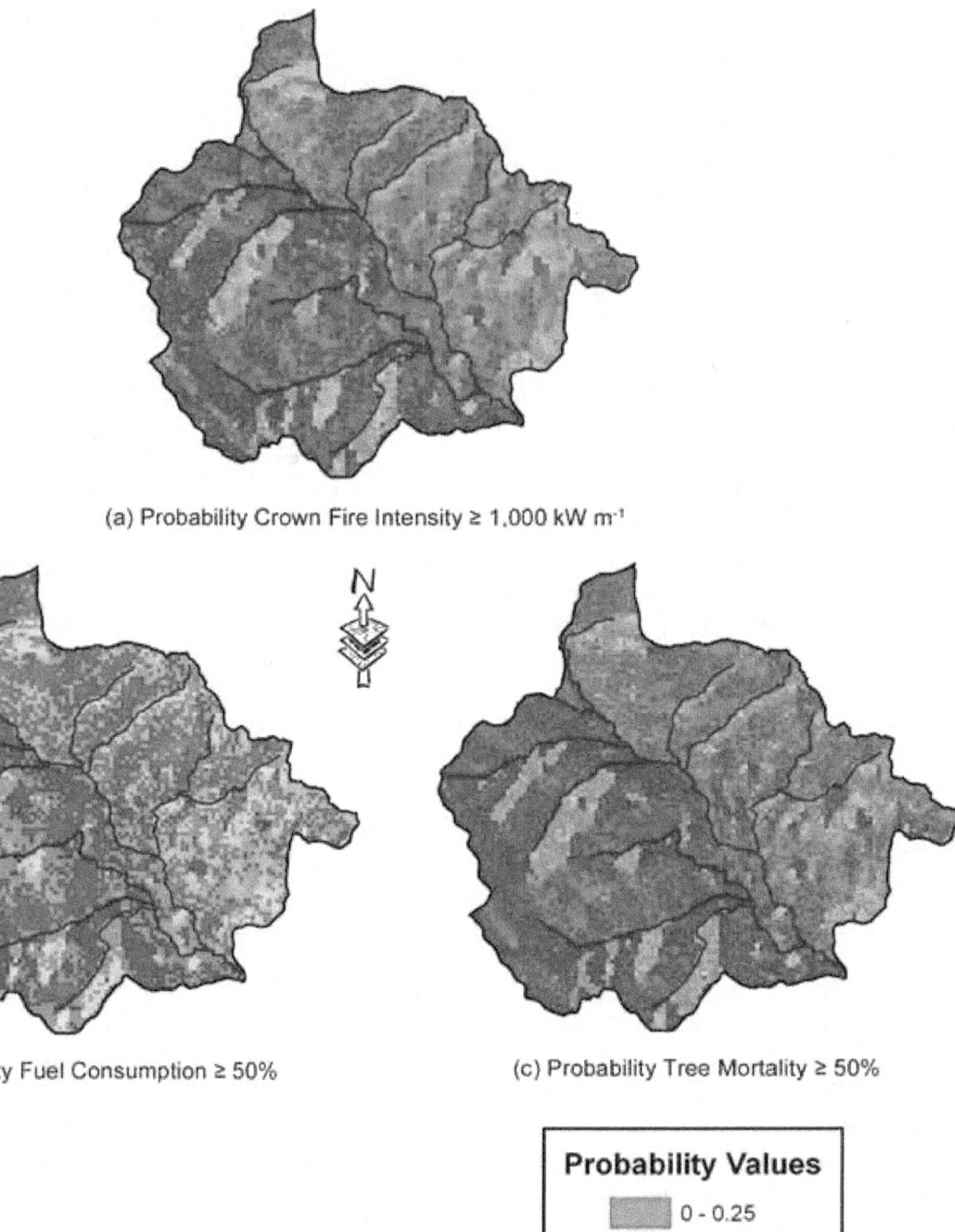

(a) Probability Crown Fire Intensity ≥ 1,000 kW m⁻¹

(b) Probability Fuel Consumption ≥ 50%

(c) Probability Tree Mortality ≥ 50%

Probability Values

	0 - 0.25
	0.25 - 0.5
	0.5 - 0.75
	0.75 - 1

0   1,750   3,500   7,000   10,500 Meters

Figure 7. Fire effects simulation maps. These maps illustrate the probability that user-designated adverse fire behavior or fire effects will occur for any day within the fire season. Fire-caused tree mortality (c) values were simulated using the NTLL map layer as input data for the Ryan-Amman tree mortality algorithm for every day during the fire season over an 18-year time period (1980 to 1997; Keane and others 2010). These maps illustrate the probability that user-designated adverse fire behavior or fire effects occur for any day within the fire season.

Future Directions

This version of NTLL is a useful first attempt at using LANDFIRE data products to create a spatially explicit, spatially consistent digital map of tree attribute data for use in fire effects modeling. Additional refinements of the LFRDB and LANDFIRE map products will improve subsequent versions of the NTLL. The NTLL can be viewed as a useful tool to simulate fire-caused tree mortality until better tree attribute map products are nationally available such as those in production by the FSVeg Spatial Analyst team (formerly INFORMS), the Nationwide Forest Imputation Study (NaFIS), and the Gradient Nearest-Neighbor mapping project for the Pacific Coast States (Ohmann 2008).

The NTLL could be improved within the framework of assigning LFRDB vegetation plots using LANDFIRE map products by making a number of changes described below.

1. The LFRDB is presently categorized by LANDFIRE mapping zone. Combining the LFRDB zone data sets into a master, national LFRDB data set would facilitate the rapid production of new tree population maps as individual maps would not need to be created for each zone. Dissolving the plot boundaries would allow plots from one zone to be included in adjacent zones where data might be lacking. And having the entire NTLL in a single global database would enable more extensive and comprehensive accuracy assessments. We did not compile the LFRDB zone data sets into a master data set as this is a large task and FAM required the NTLL to be completed in a short time frame. Moreover, LANDFIRE has determined that the LFRDB should be updated and maintained by zone.

2. New or additional map products need to be utilized, and new assignment strategies need to be developed that allow each LFRDB vegetation plot to be included in NTLL production. There were 3042 plots available in the LFRDB in Zone 19 but only 758 vegetation plots were used to create the NTLL. Utilizing each of these 3042 plots would have greatly increased the variability of tree populations across the landscape and would probably have produced a regional landscape of tree populations that better reflected the natural variation in tree populations across landscapes (Pierce and others 2009).

3. Future versions of the NTLL may be produced to represent tree attribute data such as tree size and tree density. These versions of tree-list map layers would be designed to meet specific management objectives such as timber resource management, wildlife habit management, or canopy fuel assessments.

4. Producing multiple NTLLs would likely address the pressing need for tree population data to meet different management objectives. However, the ultimate goal should be to produce a universal tree population map that meets all management needs for tree attribute data.

Theoretically, a national, universal tree population data map that adequately represents values such as tree basal area, tree height, and tree density across a landscape would produce valid results for all models that require tree attribute data. Rather than individual tree-list maps that are designed as input for specific models such as the Ryan-Amman tree mortality algorithm, a universal tree-list map would produce reliable results when used in any number of management applications, including tree growth models, wildlife habitat models, and canopy fuel models.

New mapping techniques such as those being investigated in the NaFIS may move tree population mapping closer to the goal of producing a national tree population map that has universal applications. The NaFIS is a pilot study where tree attribute data from FIA plots are being mapped using satellite imagery and nearest-neighbor techniques to meet three strategic objectives (http://blue.for.msu.edu/NAFIS/): (1) to support spatial applications such as risk assessment and natural resource planning, (2) construct forest attribute maps (tree-list map layers), and (3) distribute forest inventory data from the FIA within spatial contexts. Future versions of the NTLL will need to investigate if the developing NaFIS techniques provide better results for mapping tree-lists in acceptable time frames.

New accuracy assessment techniques should be investigated to provide additional metrics for assessing the accuracy of the NTLL. Percent correct metrics provide a simple metric for assessing accuracy but are somewhat unsatisfying. New research is needed to find metrics that truly answer the questions of how well models and/or model inputs represent real conditions. Further, a multi-scale approach for assessing NTLL accuracy needs to be developed to address NTLL accuracy at the tree, stand, regional, and map levels.

References

Arno, S. F. 1979. Forest regions of Montana. Res. Pap. INT-218. Ogden, UT: U.S. Department of Agriculture, Forest Service, Rocky Mountain Research Station. 40 p.

Berry, A. H., G. Donovan, and H. Hesseln. 2006. Prescribed burning costs and the WUI: Economic effects in the Pacific Northwest. Western Journal of Applied Forestry 21:72-78.

Bessie, W. C., and E. A. Johnson. 1995. The relative importance of fuels and weather on fire behavior in subalpine forests. Ecology 76 (3):747-762.

Blanchard, B., and R. L. Ryan. 2007. Managing the wildland-urban interface in the Northeast: Perceptions of fire risk and hazard reduction strategies. Northern Journal of Applied Forestry 24 (3):203-208.

Brown, J. K. 1985. The "unnatural fuel buildup" issue. In J. E. Lotan, B. M. Kilgore, W. C. Fischer, and R. W. Mutch, editors. Symposium and workshop on wilderness fire, Missoula, MT: U.S. Department of Agriculture, Forest Service, Intermountain Forest and Range Experiment Station: 127-128.

Brown, T. J., B. L. Hall, and A. L. Westerling. 2004. The impact of twenty-first century climate change on wildland fire danger in the western United States: An applications perspective. Climatic Change 62:365-388.

Caratti, J. F. 2006. The LANDFIRE prototype project reference database. In M. G. Rollins, and C. Frame, editors. The LANDFIRE prototype project: Nationally consistent and locally relevant geospatial data for wildland fire management. Gen. Tech. Rep. RMRS-GTR-175. Fort Collins, CO: U.S. Department of Agriculture, Forest Service Rocky Mountain Research Station: 69-98.

Cottam, C., and J. T. Curtis. 1956. The use of distance measures in phytosociological sampling. Ecology 37:451-460.

Crookston, N. L., and A. O. Finley. 2008. yaImpute: An R package for knn imputation. Journal of Statistical Software 23(10):1-16.

Dixon, Gary E. 2002. *Essential FVS: A user's guide to the forest vegetation simulator.* Internal Rep. Fort Collins, CO: U.S. Department of Agriculture, Forest Service, Forest Management Service Center. 193 p.

Ek, A. R., A. P. Robinson, P. J. Radtke, and D. K. Walters. 1997. Development and testing of regeneration imputation models for forests in Minnesota. Forest Ecology and Management 94:129-140.

Eskelson, B. N., H. Temesgen, V. LeMay, and T. M. Barrett. 2008. Comparison of stratified and non-stratified most similar neighbor imputation for estimating stand tables. Forestry 81 (2):125-134.

Eskelson, B. N., H. Temesgen, V. LeMay, and T. M. Barrett. 2009a. Estimating current forest attributes from paneled inventory data using plot-level imputation: A study from the Pacific Northwest. Forest Science 55 (1):64-71.

Eskelson, B. N., H. Temesgen, V. LeMay, T.M. Barrett, N. L. Crookston, and A.T. Hudak. 2009b. The roles of nearest neighbor methods in imputing missing data in forest inventory and monitoring databases. Scandinavian Journal of Forest Research. 24:235-246.

Ferry, G. W., R. G. Clark, R. E. Montgomery, R. W. Mutch, W. P. Leenhouts, and G. T. Zimmerman. 1995. Altered fire regimes within fire-adapted ecosystems. In Laroe, E. T., G. S. Farris, C. E. Puckett, P. D. Doran, and M. J. Mac, editors. Our living resources: A report to the nation on the distribution, abundance, and health of U.S. plants, animals, and ecosystems. Washington, DC: U.S. Department of the Interior, National Biological Service: 222-224.

Hardy, C. C. 2005. Wildland fire hazard and risk: Problems, definitions, and context. Forest Ecology and Management 211:73-82.

Haynes, R. W., T. M. Quigley, J. L. Clifford, and R. A. Gravenmier. 2001. Science and ecosystem management in the interior Columbia basin. Forest Ecology and Management 153:3-14.

Hessburg, P. F., K. M. Reynolds, R. E. Keane, K. M. James, and R. B. Salter. 2007. Evaluating wildland fire danger and prioritizing vegetation and fuels treatments. Forest Ecology and Management 247:1-17.

Holsinger, L., R. E. Keane, R. Parsons, and E. Karau. 2006. Development of biophysical gradient layers for the LANDFIRE prototype project. In M. G. Rollins, and C. Frame, editors. The LANDFIRE prototype project: Nationally consistent and locally relevant geospatial data for wildland fire management. Gen. Tech. Rep. RMRS-GTR-175. Fort Collins, CO: U.S. Department of Agriculture, Forest Service, Rocky Mountain Research Station: 99-122.

Hood, S. C., W. McHugh, K. C. Ryan, E. Reinhardt, and S. L. Smith. 2007. Evaluation of a post-fire tree mortality model for western USA conifers. International Journal of Wildland Fire 16:679-689.

Hudak, A. T., N. L.Crookston, J. S.Evans, D. E. Hall, and M. J. Falkowski. 2008. Nearest neighbor imputation of species level, plot-scale forest structure attributes from LiDAR data. Remote Sensing of the Environment. 112:2232-2245.

Jensen, M. E., and P. S. Bourgeron. 1993. Eastside forest ecosystem health assessment, vol. 11. Ecosystem management: Principles and applications. Missoula, MT: U.S. Department of Agriculture, Forest Service, Northern Region. 388 p.

Karau, E. C., and R. E. Keane. In press. Burn severity mapping using simulation modeling and satellite imagery. International Journal of Wildland Fire.

Keane, R. E., S. A. Drury, E. Karau, P. F. Hessburg, and K. M. Reynolds. 2010. A method for mapping fire hazard and risk across multiple scales and its application in fire management. Ecological Modelling 221:2-18.

Keane, R. E., L. M. Holsinger, and S. D. Pratt. 2006. Simulating historical landscape dynamics using the landscape fire succession model LANDSUM version 4.0. Gen.Tech. Rep. RMRS-GTR-171CD. Fort Collins, CO: U.S. Department of Agriculture, Forest Service, Rocky Mountain Research Station. 73 p.

Keane, R. E., M. G. Rollins, and Z. Zhu. 2007. Using simulated historical time series to prioritize fuel treatments on landscapes across the United States: The LANDFIRE prototype project. Ecological Modelling 204:485-502.

Laverty, L., and J. Williams. 2000. Protecting people and sustaining resources in fire-adapted ecosystems—A cohesive strategy. Forest Service response to GAO Report GAO/RCED 99-65. Washington DC: U.S. Department of Agriculture, Forest Service.

LeMay, V., and H. Temesgen. 2005. Comparison of nearest neighbor methods for estimating basal area and stems per hectare using aerial auxiliary variables. Forest Science 51:109-119.

Long, D. B., B. J. Losensky, and D. Bedunah. 2006. Vegetation succession modeling for the LANDFIRE prototype project. In M. G. Rollins and C. Frame, editors. The LANDFIRE prototype project: Nationally consistent and locally relevant geospatial data for wildland fire management. Gen. Tech. Rep. RMRS-GTR-175. Fort Collins, CO: U.S. Department of Agriculture, Forest Service, Rocky Mountain Research Station: 217-276.

Maltamo, M., and A. Kangas. 1998. Methods based on k-nearest neighbor regression in the prediction of basal area diameter distribution. Canadian Journal of Forest Research 28:107-1115.

Monleon, V. J., D. Azuma, and D. Gedney. 2004. Equations for predicting uncompacted crown ratio based on compacted crown ratio and tree attributes. Western Journal of Applied Forestry 19 (4):260-267.

Mouer, M., and A. R. Stage. 1995. Most similar neighbor: An improved sampling inference procedure for natural resource planning. Forest Science 41:337-359.

Mutch, R. W. 1994. Fighting fire with fire: A return to ecosystem health. Journal of Forestry 92:31-33.

Ohmann, J. L. 2008. Unpublished white paper: Nearest neighbor mapping of vegetation and "tree-lists" at landscape scales in the US–Contributions from Eric Twombly, Bob Keane, Nick Crookston, and Alan Ager. 30 September 2008. 8 p.

Ohmann, J. L., and M. J. Gregory. 2002. Predictive mapping of forest composition and structure with direct gradient analysis and nearest-neighbor imputation in coastal Oregon, U.S.A. Canadian Journal of Forest Research 32:725-741.

Pierce, K. B., Jr., J. L. Ohmann, M. C. Wimberly, M. J. Gregory, and J. S. Fried. 2009. Mapping wildland fuels and forest structure for land management: A comparison of nearest neighbor imputation and other methods. Canadian Journal of Forest Research 39:1901-1916.

Radeloff, V. C., R. B. Hammer, S. I. Stewart, J. S. Fried, S. S. Holcomb, and J. F. McKeefry. 2005. The wildland-urban interface in the United States. Ecological Applications 15:799-805.

Reams, G. A., W. D. Smith, M. H. Hansen, W. A. Bechtold, F. A. Roesch, and G. G. Moisen. 2005. The forest inventory and analysis sampling frame. In W.A. Bechtold and P.L. Patterson, editors. The enhanced forest inventory and analysis program—national sampling design and estimation procedures. Gen. Tech. Rep. SRS-80. Asheville, NC: U.S. Department of Agriculture, Forest Service, Southern Research Station: 21-36.

Reeves, M. C., K. C. Ryan, M. G. Rollins, and T. G. Thompson. 2009. Spatial fuel data products of the LANDFIRE Project. International Journal of Wildland Fire 18:250-267.

Reinhardt, E. D. 2003. Using FOFEM 5.0 to estimate tree mortality, fuel consumption, smoke production and soil heating from wildland fire. In Proceedings of the Second international wildland fire ecology and fire management congress and Fifth symposium on fire and forest meteorology. 16-20 November 2003; Orlando, FL. American Meteorological Society. P5.2

Reinhardt, E. D., and N. L. Crookston, technical editors. 2003. The fire and fuels extension to the forest vegetation simulator. Gen. Tech. Rep. RMRS-GTR-116. Ogden, UT: U.S. Department of Agriculture, Forest Service, Rocky Mountain Research Station. 218 p.

Reinhardt, E. D., R. E. Keane, and J. K. Brown. 1997. First Order Fire Effects Model: FOFEM 4.0, user's guide. Gen. Tech. Rep. INT-GTR-344. Ogden, UT: U.S. Department of Agriculture, Forest Service, Intermountain Research Station. 65 p.

Reinhardt, E. D., D. Lutes, and J. Scott. 2006. FuelCalc: A method for estimating fuel characteristics. In P. L. Andrews and B. W. Butler, compilers. Conference proceedings: Fuels management—How to measure success. 28-30 March 2006; Portland, OR. Proc. RMRS-P-41. Fort Collins, CO: U.S. Department of Agriculture, Forest Service, Rocky Mountain Research Station: 273-283.

Reynolds, K. M., P. F. Hessburg, R. E. Keane, and J. P. Menakis. 2009. Allocating fuel-treatment budgets: Recent Federal experience with decision support. Forest Ecology and Management 258:2373-2381.

Rollins, M. G. 2009. LANDFIRE: A nationally consistent vegetation, wildland fire, and fuel assessment. International Journal of Wildland Fire 18:235-249.

Rollins, M. G., and C. Frame. 2006. The LANDFIRE prototype project: Nationally consistent and locally relevant geospatial data for wildland fire management. Gen. Tech. Rep. RMRS-GTR-175. Fort Collins, CO: U.S. Department of Agriculture, Forest Service, Rocky Mountain Research Station. 417 p.

Rollins, M. G., R. E. Keane, and Z. Zhu. 2006. An overview of the LANDFIRE prototype project. In M. G. Rollins and C. Frame, editors. The LANDFIRE prototype project: Nationally consistent and locally relevant geospatial data for wildland fire management. Gen. Tech. Rep. RMRS-GTR-175. Fort Collins, CO: U.S. Department of Agriculture, Forest Service, Rocky Mountain Research Station: 5-44.

Rothermel, R. C. 1972. A mathematical model for predicting fire spread in wildland fuels. Res. Pap. INT-115. Ogden, UT: U.S. Department of Agriculture, Forest Service, Intermountain Forest and Range Experiment Station. 40 p.

Running, S. W. 2006. Is global warming causing more, larger wildfires. Science 313:927-928.

Ryan, K. C., and G. D. Amman. 1994. Interactions between fire-injured trees and insects in the greater Yellowstone area. In D.G. Dspain, editor. Plants and their environments: Proceedings of the first biennial scientific conference on the greater Yellowstone ecosystem. 16-17 September 1991. Tech. Rep. NPS/NRYELL/NRTR. Denver, CO: U.S. Department of the Interior, National Park Service, Natural Resources Publication Office: 259-271.

Ryan, K. C., and E. D. Reinhardt. 1988. Predicting postfire mortality of seven western conifers. Canadian Journal of Forest Research 18:1291-1297.

Rydberg, P. A. 1915. Phytogeographical notes on the Rocky Mountain Region IV. Forests of the subalpine and montane zones. Bulletin of the Torrey Botanical Club 42:11-25.

SAS Institute Inc., v. 9.1.3. Help and Documentation, Cary, NC: SAS Institute Inc., 2002 to 2004.

Stephens, S. L., and L. W. Ruth. 2005. Federal-fire policy in the United States. Ecological Applications 15 (2):532-542.

Temesgen, H., V. M. LeMay, K. L. Froese, and P. L. Marshall. 2003. Imputing tree-lists from aerial attributes for complex stands of south-eastern British Columbia. Forest Ecology and Management 177:277-285.

Toney, C., and M. C. Reeves. 2009. Equations to convert compacted crown ratio to uncompacted crown ratio for trees in the Interior West. Western Journal of Applied Forestry 24 (2):76-82.

Toney, C., M. Rollins, K. Short, T. Frescino, R. Tymcio, and B. Peterson. 2007. Use of FIA plot data in the LANDFIRE project. In R. E. McRoberts, A. Reams, P. C. Van Deusen, and W. H. McWillams, editors. Proceedings of the seventh annual Forest Inventory and Analysis symposium. 3-6 October, 2005; Portland, ME. Gen. Tech. Rep. WO-77. Washington, DC: U.S. Department of Agriculture, Forest Service: 309-319.

Toney, C., J. D. Shaw, and M.D. Nelson. 2009. A stem-map model for predicting tree canopy cover of Forest Inventory and Analysis (FIA) plots. In Will McWilliams, Gretchen Moisen, Ray Czaplewski, compilers. 2008 Forest Inventory and Analysis (FIA) symposium. 21-23 October 2008; Park City, UT. Proc. RMRS-P-56CD. Fort Collins, CO: U.S. Department of Agriculture, Forest Service, Rocky Mountain Research Station. 1 CD.

USDA Forest Service. 2007. Forest inventory and analysis national core field guide: Field data collection procedures for phase 2 plots. Version 4.0. Online: http://fia.fs fed. us/library/field-guides-methods-proc/docs/core_ver_4-0_10_2007_p2.pdf. Accessed: January 2010.

U.S. General Accounting Office [U.S. GAO]. 2002. Severe wildland fires: Leadership and accountability needed to reduce risks to communities and resources. Report to Congressional Requesters. GAO-02-259. Washington DC: U.S. General Accounting Office.

U.S. General Accounting Office [U.S. GAO]. 2003. Additional actions required to better identify and prioritize lands needing fuels reduction. Report to Congressional Requesters. GAO-03-805. Washington DC: U.S. General Accounting Office.

U.S. General Accounting Office [U.S. GAO]. 2005. Wildland fire management: Important progress has been made, but challenges remain to completing a cohesive strategy. Report to Congressional Requesters. GAO-02-259. Washington DC: U.S. General Accounting Office.

U.S. General Accounting Office [U.S. GAO]. 2007. Wildland fire management: Better information and a systematic process could improve agencies approach to allocating fuel reduction funds and selecting projects. Report to Congressional Requesters. GAO-07-1168. Washington DC: U.S. General Accounting Office.

U.S. General Accounting Office [U.S. GAO]/Resources, Community and Economic Development [RCED]. 1999. Western National Forests—A cohesive strategy is needed to address catastrophic wildfire threats. GAO/RCED-99-65. Washington DC: U.S. General Accounting Office.

Vogelmann, J. E., J. Kost, B. Tolk, S. Howard, S. Short, X. Chen, C. Huang, K. Pabst, and M. Rollins. In preparation. Monitoring landscape change for LANDFIRE using multi-temporal satellite imagery. U.S. Geological Survey Earth Resources Observation and Science (EROS) center, Sioux Falls, SD.

Westerling, A. L., H. G. Hidalgo, D. R. Cayan, and T. W. Swetnam. 2006. Warming and earlier spring increase in western US forest wildfire activity. Science 313:940-943.